GOVERNMENT PROCEDURES AND OPERATIONS



# NATIONAL PARK SERVICE

## ANALYSES AND TRENDS OF APPROPRIATIONS, FEES AND DONATIONS

# GOVERNMENT PROCEDURES AND OPERATIONS

Additional books in this series can be found on Nova's website under the Series tab.

Additional e-books in this series can be found on Nova's website under the eBooks tab.

GOVERNMENT PROCEDURES AND OPERATIONS

# NATIONAL PARK SERVICE

## ANALYSES AND TRENDS OF APPROPRIATIONS, FEES AND DONATIONS


CLAIRE COHEN
EDITOR



NOVINKA

*New York*

**Library of Congress Cataloging-in-Publication Data**

ISBN: 978-1-63485-819-9

*Published by Nova Science Publishers, Inc. † New York*

# CONTENTS

# PREFACE

The National Park Service (NPS) administers the National Park System, which covers 84.6 million acres of land and consists of 410 diverse units valued for their natural, cultural, and recreational importance. NPS receives appropriations in the annual Interior, Environment, and Related Agencies appropriations bill. This book discusses NPS appropriations for FY2016 and examines trends in the agency's discretionary appropriations over the past decade (FY2007-FY2016); changes in the size of the National Park System, numbers of recreation visits to the parks, and NPS staffing levels during that period; and budget data for fiscal years 2005 through 2014 on the Park Service's overall funding and fee revenue and donations.

In: National Park Service
Editor: Claire Cohen

ISBN: 978-1-63485-819-9


*Chapter 1*

# NATIONAL PARK SERVICE: FY2016 APPROPRIATIONS AND RECENT TRENDS*

***Laura B. Comay***

## SUMMARY

The National Park Service (NPS) receives appropriations in the annual Interior, Environment, and Related Agencies appropriations bill. On December 18, 2015, the President signed into law P.L. 114-113, Consolidated Appropriations Act, 2016, containing FY2016 appropriations of $2.851 billion for NPS. The enacted appropriation represents an increase of $236.6 million (9.1%) over the FY2015 enacted amount but a decrease of $196.4 million from the agency request. The Obama Administration had requested $3.048 billion in discretionary appropriations for NPS for FY2016.

Earlier, on June 18, 2015, the House Appropriations Committee reported H.R. 2822, which contained appropriations of $2.667 billion for NPS. On June 23, 2015, the Senate Appropriations Committee reported S. 1645, containing $2.729 billion for NPS. Because no regular Interior appropriations act for FY2016 was enacted prior to the end of FY2015, a series of laws (P.L. 114- 53, P.L. 114-96, and P.L. 114-100) provided

* This is an edited, reformatted and augmented version of a Congressional Research Service publication R42757, prepared for Members and Committees of Congress, dated February 23, 2016.

continuing appropriations for NPS until full-year FY2016 appropriations were enacted in P.L. 114-113.

The Obama Administration released its FY2017 budget request for NPS in February 2016. For FY2017, the agency seeks $3.101 billion in discretionary appropriations, an increase of $250.2 million (8.8%) over the enacted FY2016 appropriation. In addition to the discretionary funding, the Administration proposes $1.238 billion in mandatory appropriations for NPS for FY2017, a growth of 135.6% over NPS mandatory funding in FY2016 ($525.4 million). Some of the mandatory appropriations would require changes in authorizing law. The discretionary and mandatory requests bring the Administration's total request for NPS for FY2017 to $4.339 billion, an increase of $962.5 million (or 28.5%) over the FY2016 total of $3.376 billion. NPS states that much of the additional funding would be used to address the agency's growing backlog of deferred maintenance, in connection with NPS's centennial anniversary in 2016.

This report discusses NPS's FY2016 appropriations and examines trends in the agency's discretionary appropriations over the past decade (FY2007-FY2016). NPS appropriations rose and fell during that time. Overall, the enacted discretionary appropriation for FY2016 represented an increase of 24.0% in nominal dollars and 7.5% in inflation-adjusted dollars compared with a decade earlier (FY2007).

For most of this time, the NPS discretionary appropriation included five accounts. The largest by far is the Operation of the National Park System (ONPS) account, which supports the activities, programs, and services that form the day-to-day operations of the park system. The majority of ONPS funds are provided directly to managers of individual park units. This account grew over the decade by 11.6% in inflation-adjusted dollars. Another account, for federal and state land acquisition funding under the Land and Water Conservation Fund, grew by 135.3% in inflation-adjusted dollars. The other three accounts showed declines over the decade ranging from 8.4% to 43.7% in inflation-adjusted dollars. A sixth account, the Centennial Challenge account, was funded only in certain years.

The funding changes took place in the context of relative stability in the size of the National Park System, which grew slightly (by 0.3%) from 84.3 million to 84.6 million acres over the past 10 years. NPS staffing levels fluctuated around 20,000 and grew overall. Visits to the parks also increased over the decade, peaking at approximately 307 million visits in 2015.

# TRENDS IN NPS DISCRETIONARY APPROPRIATIONS

The sections below examine trends over the past decade (FY2007-FY2016) in NPS discretionary appropriations. The agency's discretionary appropriations rose and fell over the decade. Overall, NPS appropriations grew from $2.300 billion in FY2007 to $2.851 billion in FY2016, an increase of 24.0% in actual (nominal) dollars and 7.5% in inflation-adjusted dollars (see *Table 2* and *Figure 1*).[4] A spike in appropriations occurred in FY2009, when economic stimulus measures were enacted in P.L. 111-5, the American Recovery and Reinvestment Act of 2009. Appropriations also rose in FY2013, reflecting supplemental funding for response to Hurricane Sandy (which heavily damaged parks on the East Coast), and again in FY2016, in connection with the NPS centennial anniversary. Certain other years saw decreases in NPS appropriations.

**Table 2. NPS Discretionary Appropriations, FY2007-FY2016**

($ billions, in nominal and inflation-adjusted 2007 dollars)

| | *Appropriation in Nominal $* | *Appropriation in Inflation-Adjusted 2007 $* | *% Change Since Previous Year* | |
|---|---|---|---|---|
| | | | *Nominal* | *Inflation-Adjusted* |
| FY2007 | 2.300 | 2.300 | — | — |
| FY2008 | 2.390 | 2.342 | +3.9% | +1.8% |
| FY2009 | 3.276 | 3.172 | +37.0% | +35.5% |
| FY2010 | 2.744 | 2.634 | -16.2% | -17.0% |
| FY2011 | 2.611 | 2.457 | -4.8% | -6.7% |
| FY2012 | 2.580 | 2.383 | -1.2% | -3.0% |
| FY2013 | 2.775 | 2.521 | +7.6% | +5.8% |
| FY2014 | 2.562 | 2.288 | -7.7% | -9.2% |
| FY2015 | 2.615 | 2.304 | +2.1% | +0.7% |
| FY2016 | 2.851 | 2.473 | +9.1% | +7.4% |
| *Total Change* | *+0.551* | *+0.173* | *+24.0%* | *+7.5%* |

Source: Annual House Appropriations Committee detailed tables for NPS.

Notes: These figures exclude permanent budget authorities and generally do not reflect scorekeeping adjustments. They generally reflect rescissions and supplemental appropriations to date, including FY2009 funds from P.L. 111-5 (the American Recovery and Reinvestment Act) and FY2013 funds from P.L. 113-2 in response to Hurricane Sandy. Figures for FY2013 reflect the President's March 2013 budget sequestration and an across-the-board rescission of 0.2%. Adjustments for inflation (shown in 2007 dollars) use the GDP Chained Price Index from the White House Office of Management and Budget, Historical Tables, Table 10.1, "Gross Domestic Product and Deflators Used in the Historical Tables—1940-2021," at http://www.whitehouse.gov/omb/budget/Historicals.

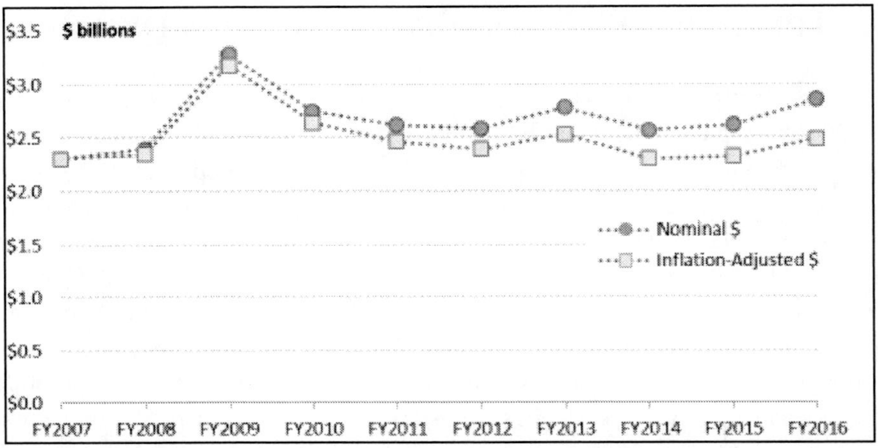


Source: Annual House Appropriations Committee detailed tables for NPS.

Notes: These figures exclude permanent budget authorities and generally do not reflect scorekeeping adjustments. They generally reflect rescissions and supplemental appropriations, including FY2009 funds from P.L. 111-5 (the American Recovery and Reinvestment Act) and FY2013 funds from P.L. 113-2 in response to Hurricane Sandy. Figures for FY2013 reflect the President's March 2013 budget sequestration and an across-the-board rescission of 0.2%. Adjustments for inflation (shown in 2007 dollars) use the GDP Chained Price Index from the White House Office of Management and Budget, Historical Tables, Table 10.1, "Gross Domestic Product and Deflators Used in the Historical Tables—1940-2021," at http://www.whitehouse.gov/omb/budget/Historicals.

Figure 1. NPS Appropriations, FY2007-FY2016. ($ billions, in nominal and inflation-adjusted 2007 dollars).

For most of the decade, NPS appropriations were spread across five accounts that cover basic park operations (Operation of the National Park System, or ONPS, account); construction and repair of infrastructure (Construction account); assistance to state, local, tribal, and private land managers (National Recreation and Preservation account); grants to states and localities for historic preservation (Historic Preservation Fund); and land acquisition by both NPS and the states (Land Acquisition and State Assistance account).[5] By far the largest share of NPS's discretionary appropriations—83.1% in FY2016—went to the ONPS account, which covers basic park operations (see *Table 1* and *Figure 2*).

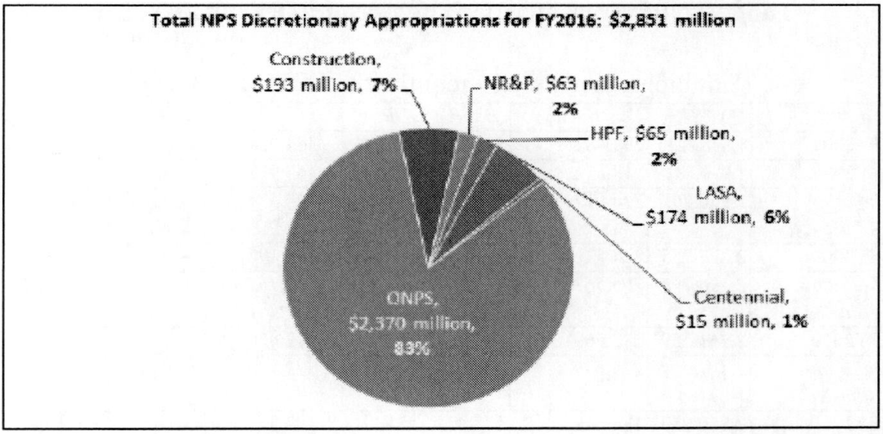


Source: P.L. 114-113, Division G, Explanatory Statement, Congressional Record, December 17, 2015, p. H10215.

Notes: ONPS = Operation of the National Park Service; NR&P = National Recreation and Preservation; HPF = Historic Preservation Fund; LASA = Land Acquisition and State Assistance. These data exclude permanent budget authorities and generally do not reflect scorekeeping adjustments. The figure for the total appropriation reflects a rescission of $28 million in Land and Water Conservation Fund (LWCF) contract authority, which is not shown in the chart.

Figure 2. NPS's FY2016 Discretionary Appropriations by Account.

In addition to these five accounts, during four years of the past decade (FY2008, FY2010, FY2015, and FY2016), Congress appropriated funds for a sixth account, the Centennial Challenge account.[6] The account consists of a matching-grant program to spur partner donations for park improvements related to the National Park System's 100th anniversary in 2016. The program received $24.6 million in FY2008, $5.0 million in FY2010 (as well as $10.0 million in carryover balances from NPS's recreational fee program), $10.0 million in FY2015, and $15.0 million in FY2016. In addition to discretionary funding, both the George W. Bush and Obama Administrations sought additional mandatory appropriations of up to $100 million annually for the Centennial Challenge account, but Congress has not established the mandatory fund. In the 114th Congress, H.R. 3556 and S. 2257 would provide mandatory appropriations for the Centennial Challenge fund (see text box above). This report reflects discretionary appropriations for the Centennial Challenge account in *Table 3*, but because the appropriations have occurred only in certain years, trends over time for this account are not discussed in the following sections.

**Table 3. NPS Appropriations by Account, FY2007-FY2016**

($ millions, in nominal and inflation-adjusted 2007 dollars)

| | *ONPS* | *Construction* | *NR&P* | *HPF* | *LASA* | *CC* | *Total*[a] |
|---|---|---|---|---|---|---|---|
| FY2007 | 1,848.421 | 297.482 | 59.295 | 60.737 | 64.024 | — | *2,299.959* |
| FY2008 | 1,970.581 | 218.522 | 67.413 | 70.385 | 68.977 | 24.610 | *2,390.488* |
| *Inflation-Adjusted* | *1,930.707* | *214.079* | *66.042* | *68.954* | *67.574* | *24.110* | *2,341.880* |
| FY2009 | 2,277.755 | 821.521 | 58.384 | 83.984 | 64.190 | — | *3,275.834* |
| *Inflation-Adjusted* | *2,205.778* | *795.561* | *56.539* | *81.330* | *62.162* | | *3,172.318* |
| FY2010 | 2,261.559 | 232.969 | 68.436 | 79.500 | 126.266 | 5.000[b] | *2,743.730* |
| *Inflation-Adjusted* | *2,171.204* | *223.639* | *65.695* | *76.316* | *121.209* | *4.800* | *2,633.850* |
| FY2011 | 2,250.050 | 184.646 | 57.245 | 54.391 | 94.810 | — | *2,611.142* |
| *Inflation-Adjusted* | *2,118.775* | *173.721* | *53.858* | *51.173* | *89.200* | | *2,456.650* |
| FY2012 | 2,236.568 | 155.366 | 59.879 | 55.910 | 101.897 | — | *2,579.620* |
| *Inflation-Adjusted* | *2,069.851* | *143.552* | *55.326* | *51.658* | *94.149* | | *2,383.460* |
| FY2013 | 2,097.261 | 453.885 | 56.747 | 100.486 | 96.567 | — | *2,774.946* |
| *Inflation-Adjusted* | *1,907.747* | *412.290* | *51.547* | *91.277* | *87.717* | | *2,520.643* |
| FY2014 | 2,236.753 | 137.461 | 60.795 | 56.410 | 98.100 | — | *2,561.519* |
| *Inflation-Adjusted* | *2,004.137* | *122.768* | *54.297* | *50.380* | *87.614* | | *2,287.720* |
| FY2015 | 2,275.773 | 138.339 | 63.117 | 56.410 | 98.960 | 10.000 | *2,614.599* |
| *Inflation-Adjusted* | *2,011.921* | *121.899* | *55.616* | *49.707* | *87.200* | *8.812* | *2,303.892* |
| FY2016 | 2,369.596 | 192.937 | 62.632 | 65.410 | 173.670 | 15.000 | *2,851.245* |
| *Inflation-Adjusted* | *2,062.111* | *167.360* | *54.329* | *56.739* | *150.647* | *13.011* | ***2,473.258*** |

Source: Annual House Appropriations Committee detailed tables for NPS.

Notes: ONPS = Operation of the National Park System account; NR&P = National Recreation and Preservation account; HPF = Historic Preservation Fund account; LASA = Land Acquisition and State Assistance account; CC = Centennial Challenge account.

These figures exclude permanent budget authorities and generally do not reflect scorekeeping adjustments. They generally reflect rescissions and supplemental appropriations to date, including FY2009 funds from P.L. 111-5 (the American Recovery and Reinvestment Act) and FY2013 funds from P.L. 113-2 in response to Hurricane Sandy. Figures for FY2013 reflect the President's March 2013 budget sequestration and an across-the-board rescission of 0.2%. Adjustments for inflation (shown in 2007 dollars) use the GDP Chained Price Index from the White House Office of Management and Budget, Historical Tables, Table 10.1,

"Gross Domestic Product and Deflators Used in the Historical Tables—1940-2021," at http://www.whitehouse.gov/omb/budget/Historicals.

[a] Totals reflect annual rescissions for LWCF contract authority of $30.0 million for FY2005-FY2013 and $28.0 million for FY2014-FY2016. Because these rescissions are not included in the amounts for individual accounts, the figures for the individual accounts do not add up to the totals shown.

[b] For FY2010, the Centennial Challenge account was titled Park Partnership Project Grants.

Several additional accounts existed for a limited time during the past decade and were either defunded or folded into other accounts. In the discussions below, calculations are adjusted to reflect the separation or merger of accounts.[7] Below the account level, funding for some individual programs, projects, or activities also shifted between accounts during the 10-year period. This report may not reflect some of the smaller such realignments that occurred throughout the decade.[8]

## Operation of the National Park System Account

Appropriations for the largest NPS account, entitled Operation of the National Park System (ONPS), increased over the decade, rising from $1.848 billion in FY2007 to $2.370 billion in FY2016 (see *Table 3* and *Figure 3*). When adjusted for inflation, this represents a growth of 11.6%. The funding supports the activities, programs, and services that form the day-to-day operations of the National Park System. Funding for these park operations grew not only in dollar amount but also as a percentage of total NPS appropriations, increasing from 80.4% of total funding in FY2007 to 83.1% in FY2016.

The majority of ONPS funds are provided directly to managers of individual park units. Activities covered under the account include visitor services, resource stewardship, park protection (including the U.S. Park Police),[9] facility operations and maintenance, and park support,[10] as well as "external administrative costs" for services provided by outside entities.[11] Among these activities, the two showing the greatest percentage growth over the decade were park support, which grew by 42.1% in inflation-adjusted dollars, and external administrative costs, which grew by 16.0% in inflation-adjusted dollars but remained the smallest activity in terms of funding.[12]

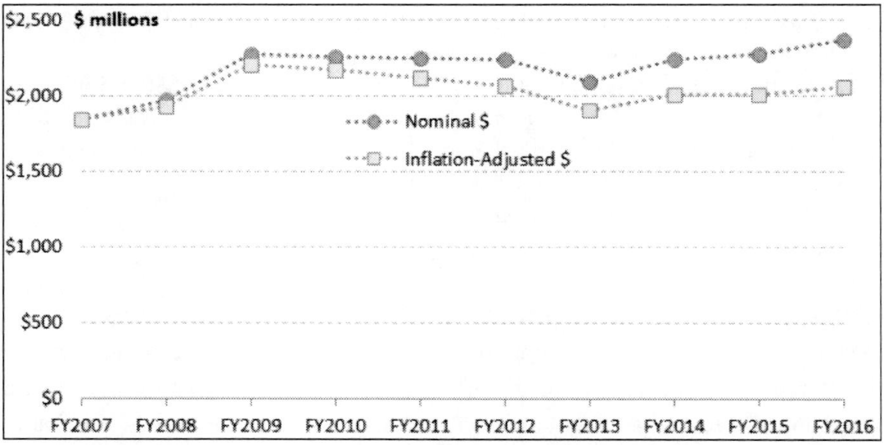


Source: Annual House Appropriations Committee detailed tables for NPS.

Notes: These figures exclude permanent budget authorities and generally do not reflect scorekeeping adjustments. They generally reflect rescissions and supplemental appropriations to date, including FY2009 funds from P.L. 111-5 (the American Recovery and Reinvestment Act) and FY2013 funds from P.L. 113-2 in response to Hurricane Sandy. Figures for FY2013 reflect the President's March 2013 budget sequestration and an across-the-board rescission of 0.2%. Adjustments for inflation (shown in 2007 dollars) use the GDP Chained Price Index from the White House Office of Management and Budget, Historical Tables, Table 10.1, "Gross Domestic Product and Deflators Used in the Historical Tables—1940-2021," at http://www.whitehouse.gov/omb/budget/Historicals.

For FY2007, the U.S. Park Police account is included in the ONPS totals to facilitate comparison with subsequent years, in which the Park Police appropriation was merged into the ONPS appropriation.

Figure 3. Appropriations for NPS's Operation of the National Park System (ONPS) Account, FY2007-FY2016. ($ millions, in nominal and inflation-adjusted 2007 dollars)

## Construction Account

The second-largest NPS account, titled Construction, funds new construction projects as well as repairs and improvements to existing facilities, among other activities. Appropriations for the account at the beginning of the decade ($297.5 million in FY2007) were higher than those at the end of the decade ($192.9 million in FY2016; see *Figure 4* and *Table 3*). Adjusting dollar amounts for inflation, this constitutes a decline of 43.7%. Construction appropriations accordingly represent a smaller portion of total NPS appropriations in FY2016 (6.8%) than they did in FY2007 (12.9%). However, this overall decline was tempered by two spikes in funding for the Construction account—one in FY2009, resulting from emergency appropriations in P.L. 111- 5, the American Recovery and Reinvestment Act of 2009, and the other in FY2013, resulting from the Hurricane Sandy supplemental appropriation in P.L. 113-2.

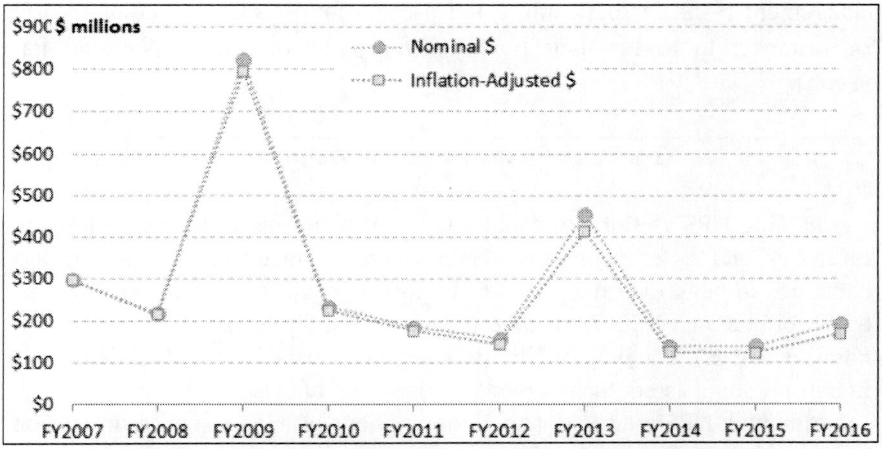


Source: Annual House Appropriations Committee detailed tables for NPS.

Notes: These figures exclude permanent budget authorities, and generally do not reflect scorekeeping adjustments. They generally reflect rescissions and supplemental appropriations to date, including FY2009 funds from P.L. 111-5, the American Recovery and Reinvestment Act, and FY2013 funds from P.L. 113-2 in response to Hurricane Sandy. Figures for FY2013 reflect the President's March 2013 budget sequestration and an across-the-board rescission of 0.2%. Adjustments for inflation (shown in 2007 dollars) use the GDP Chained Price Index from the White House Office of Management and Budget, Historical Tables, Table 10.1, "Gross Domestic Product and Deflators Used in the Historical Tables—1940–2019," at http://www.whitehouse.gov/omb/budget/ Historicals.

Figure 4. Appropriations for NPS's Construction Account, FY2007-FY2016. ($millions, in nominal and inflation-adjusted 2007 dollars)

Among the specific activities funded in the Construction account, the largest is *line-item construction and maintenance*, which covers construction of new facilities and rehabilitation and replacement of existing facilities. Projects are prioritized based on their contribution to NPS mission factors and cost-benefit considerations.[13] Funding for the line-item activity mainly declined over the decade, although it rose in FY2016. As discussed above, the overall decline was also mitigated by P.L. 111-5 stimulus funds in FY2009 and by the Hurricane Sandy supplemental in FY2013. (The portion of funding directed to the line-item subactivity in particular is not readily available for either of these appropriations.) Other activities funded in the Construction account include emergency and unscheduled construction, repair and replacement of employee housing, dam safety, equipment replacement, construction planning and program management, development of general management plans for park units, and preparation of special studies of areas (for instance, to assess their potential for inclusion in the National Park System).

**NPS Funding for Deferred Maintenance**

Despite NPS's efforts to address deferred maintenance through improved inventory and asset management, the agency's maintenance backlog has continued to build over the past decade from an estimated mid-range figure of $9.61 billion in FY2007 to an estimate of $11.93 billion for FY2015 (in nominal dollars). The bulk of NPS deferred maintenance—52% in FY2015—is in transportation assets such as roads, bridges, and tunnels.

Although NPS's discretionary appropriations provide a significant portion of the agency's funding to address deferred maintenance, such funding also comes from other sources. For example, road and bridge improvements are largely funded by allocations from the Department of Transportation. Funding to address deferred maintenance may also come through mandatory appropriations, such as fee collections.

Within NPS's discretionary appropriations, two subaccounts provide the primary funding to address deferred maintenance: the *line-item construction and maintenance* activity within the Construction account and the *facility operation and maintenance* activity within the Operation of the National Park Service account. Appropriations for line-item construction declined over the decade (-44.2% in inflation-adjusted dollars), whereas facility operation and maintenance appropriations increased (+6.4% in inflation-adjusted dollars).

For more information on NPS deferred maintenance, see National Park Service, "Planning, Design, and Construction Management: NPS Deferred Maintenance Reports," at http://www.nps.gov/subjects/plandesign construct/defermain.htm; NPS, *Budget Justifications and Performance Information, Fiscal Year 2017*, "Federal Lands Transportation Program," p. Const-79, at http://www.nps.gov/aboutus/upload/FY17-NPS-Greenbook-for-website.pdf; and CRS Report R43997, *Deferred Maintenance of Federal Land Management Agencies: FY2005-FY2014 Estimates*, by Carol Hardy Vincent.

## National Recreation and Preservation Account

The National Recreation and Preservation (NR&P) account funds NPS programs that primarily assist state, local, tribal, and private land managers with outdoor recreation planning, natural and cultural resource preservation, environmental compliance, and other activities outside the National Park System. Appropriations for the account fluctuated over the decade and rose overall in nominal dollars, from $59.3 million in FY2007 to $62.6 million in FY2016.[14] Adjusted for inflation, however, the appropriation declined by 8.4% (*Figure 5* and *Table 3*). The portion of total NPS funding used for the NR&P account also declined—from 2.6% in FY2007 to 2.2% in FY2016.

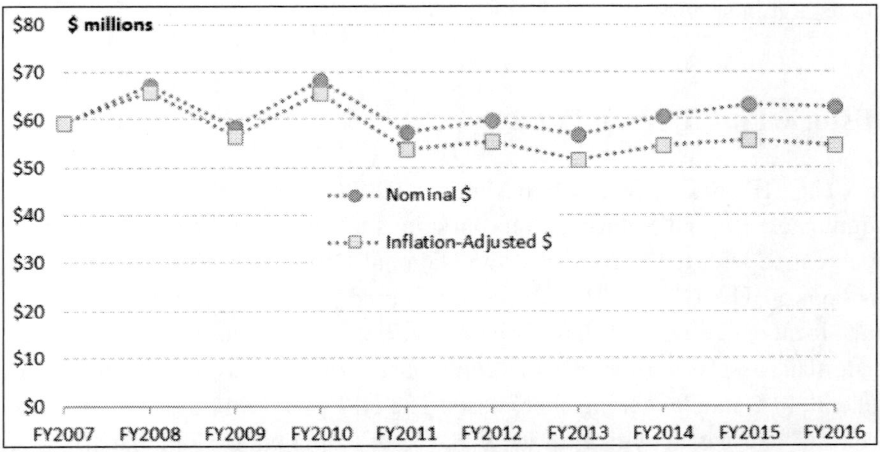


Source: Annual House Appropriations Committee detailed tables for NPS.

Notes: These figures exclude permanent budget authorities and generally do not reflect scorekeeping adjustments. They generally reflect rescissions and supplemental appropriations to date, including FY2009 funds from P.L. 111-5 (the American Recovery and Reinvestment Act) and FY2013 funds from P.L. 113-2 in response to Hurricane Sandy. Figures for FY2013 reflect the President's March 2013 budget sequestration and an across-the-board rescission of 0.2%. Adjustments for inflation (shown in 2007 dollars) use the GDP Chained Price Index from the White House Office of Management and Budget, Historical Tables, Table 10.1, "Gross Domestic Product and Deflators Used in the Historical Tables—1940-2021," at http://www.whitehouse.gov/omb/budget/Historicals. For FY2007, appropriations for the Preserve America program are included in the NR&P totals, because this program was later funded in the NR&P account.

Figure 5. Appropriations for NPS's National Recreation and Preservation (NR&P) Account, FY2007-FY2016. ($ millions, in nominal and inflation-adjusted 2007 dollars)

A variety of natural, cultural, and recreational assistance programs are funded in the NR&P account. The Heritage Partnership Program, which provides NPS assistance to national heritage areas, is the largest single program contained in the account.[15] Its appropriations grew over the decade,[16] despite Administration budget requests in recent years to reduce the heritage area appropriation by roughly half. The number of heritage areas also increased during the decade from 36 to 49. In addition, the NR&P account has included such programs as the American Battlefield Protection Program; the Rivers, Trails, and Conservation Assistance Program; the National Natural Landmarks and National Historic Landmarks Programs; the Natural Register of Historic Places; and the Preserve America Program. The account further covers international park affairs, environmental and compliance review, and grants administration.

## Historic Preservation Fund

The Historic Preservation Fund (HPF), established in 1976,[17] is administered by NPS through appropriations to the agency's HPF account. In accordance with the purposes of the National Historic Preservation Act (P.L. 89-665; 54 U.S.C. §§300101 et seq.), the fund provides grants-in-aid to state and local governments and private entities for conserving cultural and historical assets and sites. Its grants are normally awarded on a 60% federal/40% state matching share basis. The HPF has been funded by revenues from oil and gas activities on the U.S. Outer Continental Shelf. This funding authorization expired on September 30, 2015, although a balance of more than $3 billion remains in the fund and is available for appropriation.[18]

Appropriations for the HPF account varied during the decade and grew overall in nominal dollars—from $60.7 million in FY2007[19] to $65.4 million in FY2016. Adjusted for inflation, however, the appropriation declined by 6.6% (see *Figure 6* and *Table 3*). The account represented 2.6% of the total NPS appropriation in FY2007 and 2.3% in FY2016. HPF appropriations were highest in FY2013, as a result of the supplemental appropriation in response to Hurricane Sandy (P.L. 113-2), which added $47.5 million (after sequestration) to the account's regular FY2013 appropriation of $53.0 million.

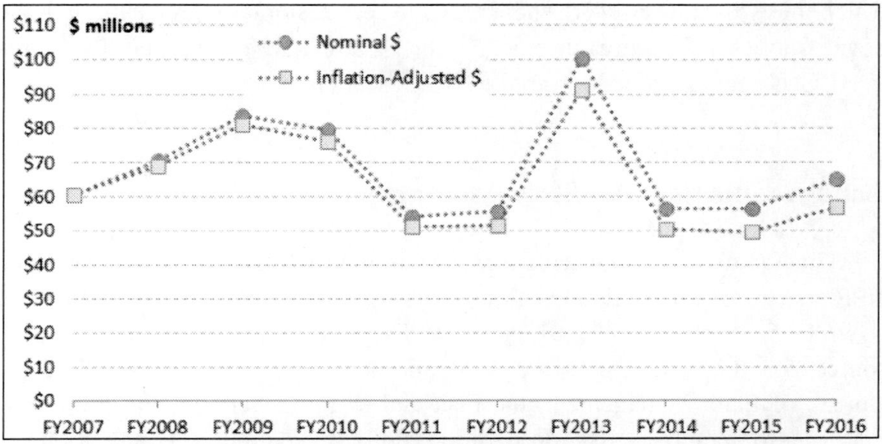


Source: Annual House Appropriations Committee detailed tables for NPS.

Notes: These figures exclude permanent budget authorities and generally do not reflect scorekeeping adjustments. They generally reflect rescissions and supplemental appropriations to date, including FY2009 funds from P.L. 111-5 (the American Recovery and Reinvestment Act) and FY2013 funds from P.L. 113-2 in response to Hurricane Sandy. Figures for FY2013 reflect the President's March 2013 budget sequestration and an across-the-board rescission of 0.2%. Adjustments for inflation (shown in 2007 dollars) use the GDP Chained Price Index from the White House Office of Management and Budget, Historical Tables, Table 10.1, "Gross Domestic Product and Deflators Used in the Historical Tables—1940-2021," at http://www.whitehouse.gov/omb/budget/Historicals. The amount for FY2007 does not include appropriations for the Preserve America program. These appropriations are instead counted with the NR&P account to facilitate comparisons with later years when the program was funded through that account.

Figure 6. Appropriations for NPS's Historic Preservation Fund (HPF) Account, FY2007-FY2016. ($ millions, in nominal and inflation-adjusted 2007 dollars)

The largest activity in the account is funding for state historic preservation offices, which rose from $37.2 million in FY2007 to $46.9 million in FY2016. Adjusted for inflation, this represents a gain of 9.4%. Tribal grants also rose from $5.4 million to $10.0 million, a growth of 59.0% after adjusting for inflation. Other program funding declined or ended during the decade. For example, the Save America's Treasures program, which helped to restore nationally significant historic structures and artifacts, was funded in varying amounts from FY2006 through FY2010, but its appropriations were eliminated in FY2011, contributing to a funding decline in that year for the overall HPF account (*Figure 6*).[20] The account also contained appropriations for grants to historically black colleges and universities (HBCUs) until FY2007,[21] after which these institutions were encouraged to seek restoration grants through the Save America's Treasures program.[22] For FY2017, NPS requested that grants to HBCUs again be funded from the NR&P account.[23]

## Land Acquisition and State Assistance

The Land Acquisition and State Assistance (LASA) account represents NPS's share of appropriations from the Land and Water Conservation Fund (LWCF; 54 U.S.C. §§200301 et seq.). The LWCF is the primary funding source for the four major federal land management agencies—NPS, the Bureau of Land Management, the Fish and Wildlife Service, and the Forest Service—to acquire lands.[24] In addition, the LWCF supports grants to states (and, through states, to localities) for outdoor recreation purposes, specifically to develop plans for outdoor recreation needs and to acquire and develop park areas. These 50/50 matching grants, administered by NPS, are generally allocated to states by formula. In recent years, a portion of the funding ($12.0 million for FY2016, of a total of $110.0 million for state assistance) also has been appropriated for a nationally competitive grant program. Overall, the LWCF is authorized at $900 million annually, but at no point in the past decade was this "full funding" appropriated.

Appropriations for the LASA account—comprising the NPS and state assistance portions of the LWCF—varied over the course of the decade and rose overall (see *Figure 7* and *Table 3*). The appropriation rose from $64.0 million in FY2007 to $173.7 million in FY2016. Adjusted for inflation, this is a growth of 135.3%. The growth is partly attributable to a significant increase in appropriations for state land acquisition in FY2016 as compared with earlier years. Altogether, the LASA account represented 2.8% of the total NPS appropriation in FY2007 and 6.1% in FY2016.

Both parts of the account—the funding for NPS land acquisition and that for assistance to states—fluctuated during the decade but grew overall. State assistance was less than $30 million annually for FY2007-FY2009, rose to roughly $40 million-$50 million annually for FY2010- FY2015, and more than doubled to $110 million for FY2016. For land acquisition by NPS, annual funding ranged between $30 million and $65 million, except in FY2010, when it rose to $86 million.

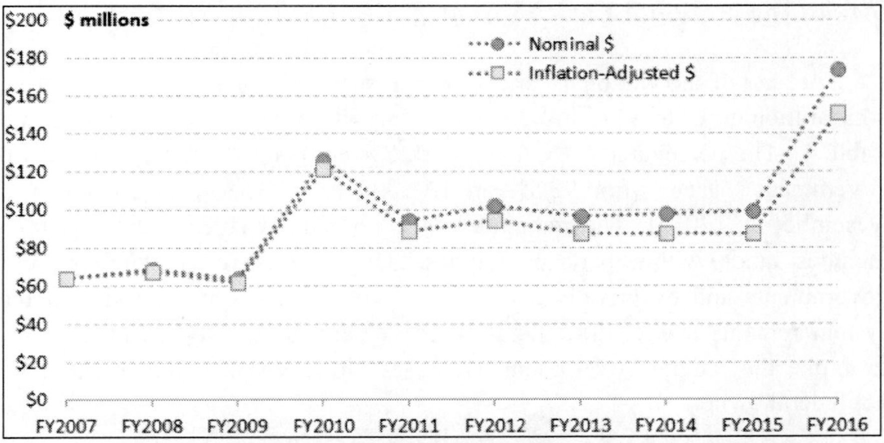


Source: Annual House Appropriations Committee detailed tables for NPS.

Notes: These figures exclude permanent budget authorities and generally do not reflect scorekeeping adjustments. They generally reflect rescissions and supplemental appropriations to date, including FY2009 funds from P.L. 111-5 (the American Recovery and Reinvestment Act) and FY2013 funds from P.L. 113-2 in response to Hurricane Sandy. Figures for FY2013 reflect the President's March 2013 budget sequestration and an across-the-board rescission of 0.2%. Adjustments for inflation (shown in 2007 dollars) use the GDP Chained Price Index from the White House Office of Management and Budget, Historical Tables, Table 10.1, "Gross Domestic Product and Deflators Used in the Historical Tables—1940-2021," at http://www.whitehouse.gov/omb/budget/Historicals.

Figure 7. Appropriations for NPS's Land Acquisition and State Assistance (LASA) Account, FY2007-FY2016. ($ millions, in nominal and inflation-adjusted 2007 dollars)

## NPS Appropriations in Context

Changes in NPS appropriations can be considered in the context of the National Park System's size, the number of visits to the parks, and NPS staffing levels, among other factors. Over the past decade, the size of the National Park System has remained relatively stable, growing by 0.3%. Visitation peaked in 2014 and 2015, and it was generally higher in the second part of the decade than the first. (However, in 2013 visitor numbers dropped, due partly to park closures after Hurricane Sandy and the October 2013 government shutdown.) Staffing levels fluctuated around 20,000 during the past 10 years.

## Size of the National Park System

The size of the National Park System rose slightly over the decade, from 84.3 million acres to 84.6 million acres, a growth of 0.3%. (See Figure 8 and Table 4.) The percentage of National Park System lands owned by the federal government[25] grew from 93.5% in FY2007 to 95.3% in FY2016 (as of December 31, 2015). The remainder—the nonfederal land in the system—includes lands within park boundaries that are owned by state or local governments and by private landowners. Even when the overall size of the system remains stable, the federal share of park lands may increase if, for example, the federal government purchases "inholdings" within parks from nonfederal owners.

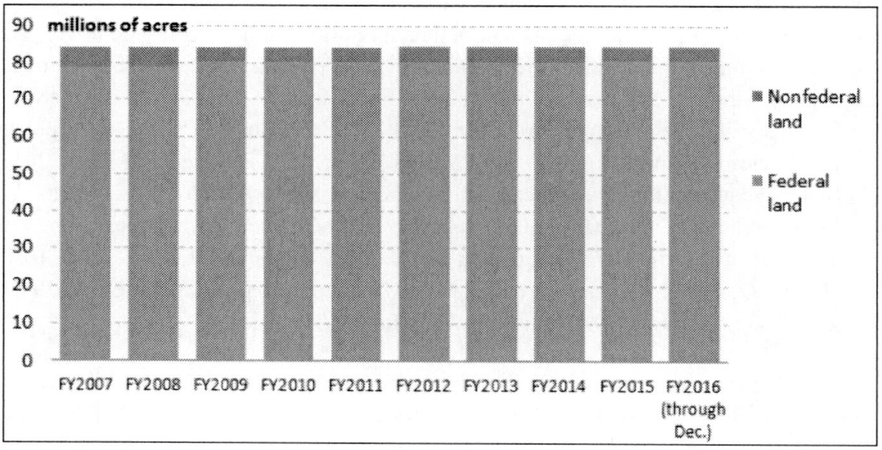


Source: NPS Land Resources Division, annual summaries of acreage, available on NPS Stats web page at https:// irma.nps.gov/Stats/Reports/National.

Notes: Federal Land category includes NPS Fee Acres, Less Than Fee Acres, and Other Federal Fee Acres. Nonfederal Land category includes Other Public Acres and Private Acres.

Figure 8. Size of the National Park System, FY2007-FY2016. (in millions of acres, through December 31, 2015)

Although the overall size of the National Park System did not change significantly, 20 new units were added to the system in the FY2007-FY2016 period (to date).[26] Other acreage changes resulted from boundary adjustments in existing parks.

**Table 4. Size of the National Park System, FY2007-FY2016**

(in millions of acres, through December 31, 2015)

| | Federal Land | Nonfederal Land | Total Acreage |
|---|---|---|---|
| FY2007 | 78.846 | 5.477 | 84.322 |
| FY2008 | 78.855 | 5.476 | 84.331 |
| FY2009 | 80.438 | 3.938 | 84.375 |
| FY2010 | 80.518 | 3.863 | 84.381 |
| FY2011 | 80.485 | 3.900 | 84.385 |
| FY2012 | 80.384 | 4.039 | 84.423 |
| FY2013 | 80.473 | 4.007 | 84.479 |
| FY2014 | 80.466 | 4.012 | 84.478 |
| FY2015 | 80.598 | 4.021 | 84.616 |
| FY2016 (through Dec. 2015) | 80.603 | 4.014 | 84.618 |

Source: NPS, Land Resources Division, annual summaries of acreage, available on NPS Stats web page at https://irma.nps.gov/Stats/Reports/National.

Notes: Federal Land category includes NPS Fee Acres, Less Than Fee Acres, and Other Federal Fee Acres. Nonfederal Land category includes Other Public Acres and Private Acres.

## Visits to the National Parks

Numbers of recreational visits to the National Park System varied over the past 10 years but were generally higher toward the end of the decade. The highest numbers of visits were in 2014 (292.8 million visits) and 2015 (307.2 million visits; see *Figure 9* and *Table 5*). Visits at the end of the decade were 11.5% higher than at the beginning.[27] However, visitor numbers dipped in 2013, due in part to Hurricane Sandy, which forced closures at East Coast park units,[28] and to the government shutdown of October 2013.[29]

**Table 5. Annual Recreational Visits to the National Park System, 2007-2016**

(total visits by calendar year, through January 2016)

| Year | Number of Visits (in millions) | Year | Number of Visits (in millions) |
|---|---|---|---|
| 2007 | 275.582 | 2012 | 282.766 |
| 2008 | 274.853 | 2013 | 273.631 |
| 2009 | 285.580 | 2014 | 292.800 |
| 2010 | 281.304 | 2015 | 307.247 |
| 2011 | 278.939 | 2016 (thr. Jan.) | 12.874 |

Source: NPS, NPS Stats, at https://irma.nps.gov/Stats/Reports/National.

Notes: The figure for 2016 shows visits through January 2016. For comparison with the previous year, visits through January 2015 were slightly lower at 12.190.

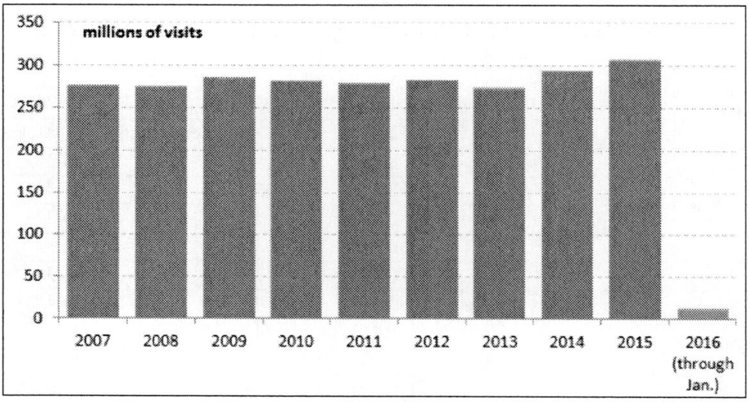


Source: National Park Service, NPS Stats, at https://irma.nps.gov/Stats/Reports/National.

Figure 9. Annual Recreational Visits to the National Park System, 2007-2016. (total visits in millions, by calendar year, through January 2016)

## National Park Service Staffing

NPS's full-time equivalent (FTE) staffing level during the past decade ranged from a low of 19,832 in FY2007 to a high of 22,211 in FY2010 (*Figure 10* and *Table 6*). Measured across the decade, staff size grew from 19,832 in FY2007 to an estimated 21,635 for FY2016, an increase of 9.1%.

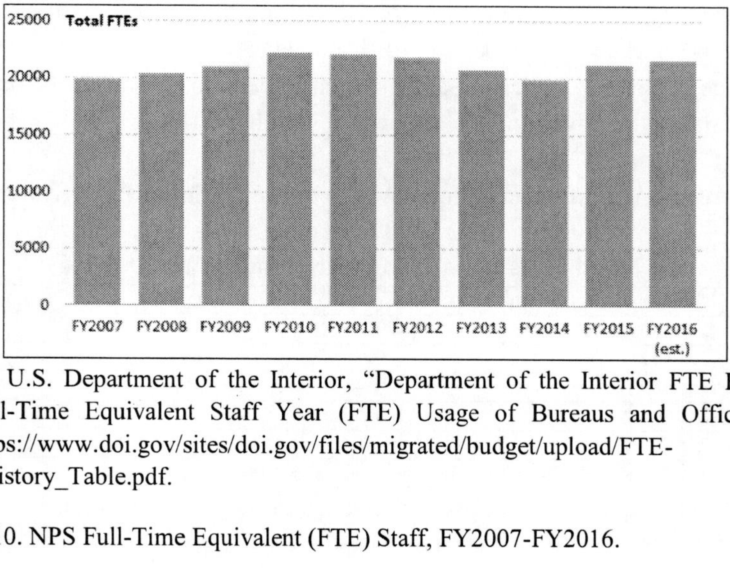


Source: U.S. Department of the Interior, "Department of the Interior FTE History: Full-Time Equivalent Staff Year (FTE) Usage of Bureaus and Offices," at https://www.doi.gov/sites/doi.gov/files/migrated/budget/upload/FTE-_History_Table.pdf.

Figure 10. NPS Full-Time Equivalent (FTE) Staff, FY2007-FY2016.

**Table 6. NPS Full-Time Equivalent (FTE) Staff, FY2007-FY2016**

| Year | Number of FTEs | Year | Number of FTEs |
|---|---|---|---|
| FY2007 | 19,832 | FY2012 | 21,830 |
| FY2008 | 20,301 | FY2013 | 20,720 |
| FY2009 | 20,991 | FY2014 | 19,894 |
| FY2010 | 22,211 | FY2015 | 21,164 |
| FY2011 | 22,051 | FY2016 (est.) | 21,635 |

Source: U.S. Department of the Interior, "Department of the Interior FTE History: Full-Time Equivalent Staff Year (FTE) Usage of Bureaus and Offices," at http://www.doi.gov/budget/upload/FTE-_History_Table.pdf.

## CONCLUSION

P.L. 114-113 provided $2.851 billion in discretionary appropriations for NPS for FY2016. For FY2017, the agency has requested discretionary appropriations of $3.101 billion, an 8.8% increase over the enacted FY2016 appropriation. Much of the additional funding would be for activities associated with the agency's centennial anniversary in 2016, especially to address deferred maintenance in the context of the centennial.

NPS also requested a significant increase in its mandatory appropriations for FY2017, some of which would require changes in authorizing law. Bills in the 114th Congress would provide some of these requested mandatory appropriations.

Over the past decade (FY2007-FY2016), NPS discretionary appropriations rose by 24.0% in nominal dollars and 7.9% in inflation-adjusted dollars. In general, the proportion of NPS funding devoted to basic park operations—the Operation of the National Park System account—increased over the decade, as did the proportion for land acquisition, while funding for other areas in the NPS portfolio, including construction, declined.

The funding changes took place in the context of a park system of stable size, with a staffing level that hovered around 20,000. Visits to the parks were generally higher in the second half of the decade than the first and peaked in 2015 at approximately 307 million visits.

## End Notes

[1] National Park Service (NPS), Budget Justifications and Performance Information, Fiscal Year 2016, p. Overview-4, at http://www.nps.gov/aboutus/upload/FY-2016-Greenbook.pdf.

[2] The House measure was debated on the floor in June and July 2015. Amendments were offered, including those concerning the sale of the Confederate flag by NPS concessioners, the flag's display at national cemeteries administered by NPS, and its purchase and display at park units generally. Further action was not anticipated until agreement could be reached on the Confederate flag issues. For more information, see CRS Insight IN10313, Display of the Confederate Flag at Federal Cemeteries, by Laura B. Comay and Barbara Salazar Torreon.

[3] For more on NPS's deferred maintenance backlog, estimated for FY2015 at $11.93 billion, see CRS Report R43997, Deferred Maintenance of Federal Land Management Agencies: FY2005-FY2014 Estimates, by Carol Hardy Vincent.

[4] Changes in appropriations over time may be measured in actual dollars (also called nominal or current dollars) or in dollar amounts that are adjusted for inflation (known as real, constant, or inflation-adjusted dollars). The latter measure is useful for gauging the relative impact of appropriations over the long term. For example, although NPS's discretionary appropriations of $2.615 billion in FY2015 were higher in nominal dollars than the $2.256 billion appropriated in FY2006, the FY2015 figure bought only the amount of goods and services that $2.251 billion would have purchased in FY2006. In this sense, the FY2015 appropriation represented a decline in NPS spending power compared with FY2006. Several different indexes measure inflation and allow for calculations of inflation-adjusted dollar amounts. This report uses the GDP Chained Price Index from the White House Office of Management and Budget, Historical Tables, Table 10.1, "Gross Domestic Product and Deflators Used in the Historical Tables—1940- 2021," at http://www.whitehouse.gov/omb/budget/Historicals. For more information on measuring inflation, see CRS Report RL30344, Inflation: Causes, Costs, and Current Status, by Marc Labonte.

[5] The Land Acquisition and State Assistance account constitutes NPS's portion of appropriations from the Land and Water Conservation Fund (LWCF). The LWCF is the principal source of funding used by four federal land management agencies—NPS, the Bureau of Land Management, the Forest Service, and the Fish and Wildlife Service— for land acquisition for outdoor recreation. In addition, the LWCF provides grants to states for outdoor recreation purposes. These grants are administered through NPS. For more information on the LWCF, see CRS Report RL33531, Land and Water Conservation Fund: Overview, Funding History, and Issues, by Carol Hardy Vincent.

[6] The account was titled Centennial Challenge in FY2008, FY2015, and FY2016, but it was called Park Partnership Project Grants in FY2010.

[7] See the discussions below for specific examples.

[8] For example, in FY2007, funding for three museums moved from the National Recreation and Preservation account to the Operation of the National Park System (ONPS) account, and funding for the Harpers Ferry Center moved from the ONPS account to the Construction account.

[9] Prior to FY2008, the U.S. Park Police—a uniformed law-enforcement entity providing protection to park sites in the metropolitan areas of San Francisco, New York City, and Washington, DC—received funding under a separate U.S. Park Police account. In this report, ONPS appropriations totals for FY2007 include the Park Police account to provide consistency with subsequent years in which Park Police funding was merged into the ONPS account.

[10] The park support activity includes administering, managing, and supporting the operations of park units.

[11] These external administrative costs include employee compensation payments, unemployment compensation payments, centralized information technology costs, telecommunications, postage, space rental from the General Services Administration, and departmental program charges.

[12] These calculations use funding amounts from annual House Appropriations Committee detailed tables for NPS. It is difficult to calculate exact percentage growth or decline for three of the activities—resource stewardship, visitor services, and park protection (including the U.S. Park Police)—because an account realignment in FY2010 significantly reorganized programs within these areas. However, these three activities combined show a slight growth (+2.0% in inflation-adjusted dollars) between FY2007 and FY2016. Funding for facility operations and maintenance also grew (+6.4% in inflation-adjusted dollars) in this period.

[13] A fuller description of NPS's two-tier priority system is in the agency's FY2017 budget justification, p. Const-8, at http://www.nps.gov/aboutus/upload/FY17-NPS-Greenbook-for-website.pdf.

[14] To facilitate multiyear comparisons, the FY2007 total for the National Recreation and Preservation (NR&P) account includes appropriations for the Preserve America program, which was shifted to this account beginning in FY2008.

[15] National heritage areas are established by Congress but are not federally managed, and they are not part of the National Park System. For more on national heritage areas, see CRS Report RL33462, Heritage Areas: Background, Proposals, and Current Issues, by Carol Hardy Vincent and Laura B. Comay.

[16] In inflation-adjusted dollars, the FY2016 appropriation for heritage area partnerships was 29.4% higher than the FY2007 appropriation.

[17] The fund was established in an amendment to the National Historic Preservation Act of 1966 (P.L. 94-422, amending P.L. 89-665; 54 U.S.C. §§300101 et seq.).

[18] Office of Management and Budget, Budget of the United States Government, Fiscal Year 2017, Appendix, p. 700, at https://www.whitehouse.gov/sites/default/files/omb/ budget/fy 2017/assets/int.pdf. Bills in the 114th Congress (H.R. 2817, S. 556, S. 2012, S. 2089) would extend the funding authorization.

[19] The amount shown for FY2007 does not include appropriations for the Preserve America program. See footnote 14.

[20] Although the Save America's Treasures program has not been funded in recent years, it continues to administer existing grants.

[21] See NPS, Budget Justifications and Performance Information, Fiscal Year 2008, p. HPF-11, at http://home.nps.gov/ applications/budgetweb/downloads/fy_2008_greenbook.pdf. As of FY2008, the Historically Black Colleges and Universities (HBCU) program also had $4.3 million in unobligated funding to continue to award to HBCUs, although new funds were not being appropriated.

[22] The Historic Preservation Fund (HPF) account also included appropriations for the Preserve America matching-grant program in FY2007, but in this report its appropriations are counted in the NR&P account, where the program was later funded. Figure 6 thus does not reflect any funding for this program. The program supported historic preservation efforts through heritage tourism, education, and historic preservation planning. It received no funding after FY2010.

[23] The agency has requested $3.0 million for grants to HBCUs for preservation of sites and stories relating to civil rights and the African-American experience.

[24] For more information on the LWCF, see CRS Report RL33531, Land and Water Conservation Fund: Overview, Funding History, and Issues, by Carol Hardy Vincent. In addition to the state grants and federal land acquisition grants discussed here, a portion of the LWCF also has been used to fund other programs.

[25] Almost all of the system's federally owned lands are directly administered by NPS. However, the federally owned portion of the system also includes some NPS "less than fee" acres (e.g., conservation easements or rights-of-way) and some lands managed by other federal agencies, such as the Bureau of Reclamation, the Forest Service, or the Fish and Wildlife Service. Taken together, these lands amount to about 1% of the federally owned portion of the system.

[26] These units are the Sand Creek Massacre National Historic Site (CO), Port Chicago Naval Magazine National Memorial (CA), River Raisin National Battlefield Park (MI), President William Jefferson Clinton Birthplace Home National Historic Site (AR), Martin Luther King Jr. Memorial (DC), Fort Monroe National Monument (VA), Paterson Great Falls National Historical Park (NJ), Cesar E. Chavez National Monument (CA), Harriet Tubman Underground Railroad National Historical Park (MD), First State National Historical Park (DE), Charles Young Buffalo Soldiers National Monument (OH), Tule Springs Fossil Beds National Monument (NV), World War I Memorial (DC), Valles Caldera National Preserve (NM), Blackstone River Valley National Historical Park (MA and RI), Pullman National Monument (IL), Honouliuli National Monument (HI), Waco Mammoth National Monument (TX), Manhattan Project National Historical Park (TN, NM, and WA), and Castle Mountains National Monument (CA). A list of recent additions to the National Park System can be found at NPS, Recent Changes in the National Park System, at http://www.nps.gov/aboutus/news/upload/ChangesintheNationalParkSystem410.pdf.

[27] This compares the 2015 visitor total with that for 2007, since 2015 is the most recent year with complete data.

[28] The storm, which struck the East Coast in October 2012, closed nearly 70 park units, in some cases for months. These included heavily visited sites such as the Statue of Liberty, which remained closed through July 2013.

[29] In October 2013, the month of the government shutdown, visitation dropped by 6.4 million compared to the previous October. The total decrease for 2013 compared to 2012 was 9.1 million. See NPS, 2013 National Park Visitor Spending Effects: Economic Contributions to Local Communities, States, and the Nation, Natural Resource Report NPS/NRSS/EQD/NRR—2014/824, July 2014, pp. 2-3, at http://www.nature.nps.gov/socialscience/docs/ NPSVSE2013_final_nrss.pdf.

In: National Park Service
Editor: Claire Cohen

ISBN: 978-1-63485-819-9


*Chapter 2*

# NATIONAL PARK SERVICE: REVENUES FROM FEES AND DONATIONS INCREASED, BUT SOME ENHANCEMENTS ARE NEEDED TO CONTINUE THIS TREND*

*United States Government Accountability Office*

## WHY GAO DID THIS STUDY

The Park Service manages 409 park units that cover 84 million acres. Park Service funding is generally composed of annual appropriations along with revenues from recreation fees, commercial service fees, and philanthropic donations. GAO was asked to review the Park Service's collection of these fees and donations.

This report examines the Park Service's (1) overall funding trends for fiscal years 2005 through 2014; (2) trends in revenues from fees and donations; and (3) efforts to increase revenues and donations, and factors that affected these efforts. To conduct this work, GAO analyzed budget data for fiscal years 2005 through 2014 on the Park Service's overall funding and fee revenue and donations. GAO also reviewed laws, examined Park Service reports, and interviewed agency officials and stakeholders, such as nonprofit partners and concessioners.

---

* This is an edited, reformatted and augmented version of the United States Government Accountability Office publication, GAO-16-166, dated December 2015.

## What GAO Recommends

Congress should consider amending FLREA so that the federal agencies that charge recreation fees can determine whether to adjust the price of a senior pass. GAO also recommends that the Department of the Interior direct the Park Service to revise its guidance to periodically review entrance fees and direct park units to provide information on their decisions to not increase fees. Interior concurred with the recommendations.

## What GAO Found

The National Park Service's (Park Service) total funding did not keep pace with inflation for fiscal years 2005 through 2014, even as fees and donations increased. Total funding increased in nominal dollars from $2.7 billion to $3.1 billion (15 percent) during this period, but declined by 3 percent after adjusting for inflation. Annual appropriations, which comprised about 88 percent of total funding on average, declined 8 percent after adjusting for inflation. Fees, donations, and other funding sources, which accounted for the remainder, increased 39 percent after adjusting for inflation.

Revenues from fees and donations grew for fiscal years 2005 through 2014 to varying degrees. Specifically, revenues from recreation fees, which include entrance and amenity fees for facilities such as campsites, increased from about $148 million to $186 million (26 percent). Revenues from fees from concessions operations, which comprise the vast majority of commercial service fees, nearly tripled from almost $29 million to $85 million. Meanwhile, cash donations from philanthropic sources fluctuated, ranging from $19.5 million in fiscal year 2011 to $94.7 million in fiscal year 2014.

The Park Service has efforts under way to increase revenues from fees and donations, but certain factors limit these efforts. For recreation fees, the Park Service updated its fee schedule, and several park units increased entrance and amenity fees. However, the Federal Lands Recreation Enhancement Act (FLREA) does not give the Park Service and other agencies that charge recreation fees the authority to adjust the price of a lifetime senior pass, which has been $10 since 1993. GAO's guide on user fees states that federal agencies should regularly review fees and make changes if warranted. Without the authority to modify the price of the senior pass, the Park Service is limited in its ability to increase revenue from this fee. In addition, Park Service guidance on recreation fees directs the agency to ensure its fees are set at a reasonable level, but does not call for periodic reviews of these fees, and the agency has no plans to do so. The agency also does not require park units to provide information on decisions to not change their fees or deviate from the fee schedule because decisions about raising fees are left to the park units. As a result, the Park Service is missing opportunities to ensure that its entrance fees are reasonable. To increase commercial service revenues, the Park Service increased minimum franchise fees that concessioners pay, and some park units have developed leasing programs. Several factors, such as limited competition for some concessions contracts, complicate efforts to increase these fees. For philanthropic donations, the Park Service has launched fundraising and public outreach campaigns in conjunction with its centennial anniversary in 2016 and has modified fundraising policies to increase donation opportunities. According to agency officials, several factors hamper the agency's ability to increase donations, such as projects that need funding are not always attractive to donors.

## ABBREVIATIONS

| | |
|---|---|
| Concessions Act | National Park Service Concessions Management Improvement Act of 1998 |
| C&O | Chesapeake and Ohio |
| FLREA | Federal Lands Recreation Enhancement Act |
| Foundation | National Park Foundation |
| IRS | Internal Revenue Service |
| LSI | Leaseholder Surrender Interest |
| MAX | MAX Information System |
| OMB | Office of Management and Budget |
| Park Service | National Park Service |

***

December 15, 2015

The Honorable Lisa Murkowski
Chairman
Committee on Energy and Natural Resources
United States Senate

The Honorable Michael Enzi
United States Senate

The National Park Service (Park Service)—within the Department of the Interior—manages 409 park units that cover 84 million acres across all 50 states, the District of Columbia, and some territories. These park units, which include national parks, historic sites, monuments, recreation areas, and battlefields, received 293 million visits in 2014. In recent years, reports prepared by the Park Service and stakeholder groups have highlighted challenges the Park Service faces—including fiscal challenges. The Park Service has reported that its funding does not cover the full cost of its mission to preserve the park units for current and future generations to enjoy. In 2006, we reported that the Park Service faced a backlog of about $5 billion for the buildings, trails, and artifacts it is responsible for maintaining,[1] and in a 2013 testimony before Congress, the Director of the Park Service stated that about $250 million in additional annual funding was needed to keep this maintenance backlog from growing. As of September 30, 2014, the Park Service estimated its maintenance backlog had grown to about $11.5 billion.[2]

Funding for the Park Service is generally composed of annual appropriations along with revenues generated from fees and donations that the Park Service is authorized to collect and use.[3] Fees include recreation fees—primarily entrance and amenity fees—and commercial service fees paid by private companies that provide services, such as operating lodges and retail stores in park units. The Park Service can also receive cash and in-kind donations from nonprofit partner groups, known as friends groups and cooperating associations. In addition, the Park Service benefits from individuals who volunteer their time at individual park units.

In a 2013 testimony before Congress, the Director of the Park Service said that the agency was reassessing its commercial service fees and undertaking other efforts to generate additional revenue for the agency. With the Park Service approaching its centennial in 2016, policymakers and others have proposed additional ways to help the Park Service handle its fiscal challenges, including for the Park Service to increase revenues from fees and donations.

You asked us to review funding for the Park Service, including the fees and donations it is authorized to collect. This report examines (1) general trends in funding for the Park Service for fiscal years 2005 through 2014; (2) the trends in the Park Service's revenues from recreation and commercial service fees and donations from philanthropic sources for fiscal years 2005 through 2014; and (3) the Park Service's efforts to increase fee revenues and donations, and factors, if any, that may affect these efforts.

To examine general funding trends for the Park Service for fiscal years 2005 through 2014, we obtained and analyzed data on the Park Service from the Office of Management and Budget (OMB) MAX Information System (MAX).[4] Data reported in OMB MAX are subject to review and checks through OMB to help ensure consistency of the data, and we determined these data were sufficiently reliable for our purposes. We analyzed these data in both nominal and inflation adjusted terms.[5] We also examined Park Service budget documents, including its annual budget justifications and spoke with Park Service officials at headquarters, regional offices, and park units to better understand these trends.

To examine trends in fee revenues and donations for the Park Service for fiscal years 2005 through 2014, we analyzed OMB MAX data along with other data on these funding sources we received from the Park Service. We used the OMB MAX data to examine the trends at a national level, and we used the data from the Park Service to examine trends at the park unit level. We also interviewed Park Service officials at headquarters, regional offices, and park units to better understand the trends we identified in the data. To determine the reliability of the Park Service's data, we spoke with agency officials that were familiar with these data, reviewed relevant documentation, and compared these data to data from OMB MAX. We generally found these data to be sufficiently reliable for our purposes. The exception is the park unit level data on philanthropic donations, which we found to have certain limitations, and we identify these limitations in our use of these data.

To examine the Parks Service's efforts to increase fee revenues and donations and any factors that may affect these efforts, we examined Park Service documents and interviewed agency officials at the headquarters, regional, and park unit levels. We compared this information with relevant laws and agency policies, as well as GAO's design guide for federal user fees[6] and *Standards for Internal Control in the Federal Government.*[7] We interviewed officials at 23 park units in person and contacted officials from another 8 park units by phone and asked about their experiences with these funding sources. In selecting parks, we included a range of park units that varied by certain characteristics, including number of visitors and type (i.e., scenic vs. historical), and we interviewed officials from at least 1 park unit in all 7 of the Park Service's regions. We also interviewed stakeholders, including concessioners and nonprofit partners. We selected these stakeholders because of their affiliation with parks in our review or because they would be able to provide other perspectives on these revenue sources. The views from these interviews are not generalizable to all parks, concessioners, and nonprofit partners, but they were used to provide a range of perspectives on Park Service's efforts. Appendix I contains a more detailed description of our objectives, scope, and methodology.

We conducted this performance audit from October 2014 to December 2015 in accordance with generally accepted government auditing standards. Those standards require that we plan and perform the audit to obtain sufficient, appropriate evidence to provide a reasonable basis for our findings and conclusions based on our audit objectives. We believe that the evidence obtained provides a reasonable basis for our findings and conclusions based on our audit objectives.

## BACKGROUND

The National Park Service Organic Act of 1916 established the Park Service within the Department of the Interior to promote and regulate the use of the National Park System with the purpose of conserving the scenery, natural and historic objects, and wildlife therein and to leave them unimpaired for the enjoyment of future generations.[8] The Park Service manages its responsibilities through its headquarters office located in Washington, D.C., seven regional offices, and 409 individual park units that are part of the system. Park unit types include national parks, such as Yellowstone and Great Smoky Mountains; national historic parks, such as Valley Forge and the Chesapeake and Ohio Canal; national battlefields, such as Antietam and Fort Necessity; national historic sites, such as Ford's Theatre and Theodore Roosevelt's birthplace; national monuments, such as Muir Woods and the Statue of Liberty; national preserves, such as the Yukon-Charley Rivers and Big Cypress; national recreation areas, such as Lake Mead and the Chattahoochee River, and national lakeshores, such as Sleeping Bear Dunes and the Apostle Islands.

Funding for the Park Service is composed of two sources: (1) annual appropriations and (2) fees, donations, and other funding sources.

**Annual appropriations.** The Park Service generally receives funding through annual appropriations acts, which provide funds used by park units or applicable entities, such as states and local governments, in the following five accounts:[9]

- **Operation of the National Park System.** Provides base funding for the operation of park units and for Park Service-wide programs. This funding is used by park units for visitor services, park protection, and maintenance projects, among other things.
- **National Recreation and Preservation.** Supports programs that assist state, local, and tribal governments, and private organizations with outdoor recreation, preservation, and environmental compliance.
- **Historic Preservation Fund.** Provides grants to state, territorial, and tribal governments and certain private groups for preserving historical and cultural resources.
- **Construction.** Supports planning and implementation of major rehabilitation and replacement projects at park units, along with unplanned, emergency construction projects.
- **Land Acquisition and State Assistance.** Uses funding from the Land and Water Conservation Fund[10] to support Park Service land acquisition activities and provide grants to state and local governments for the purchase of land for recreation activities.

**Fees, donations, and other funding sources.** The Park Service collects and uses funds from fees, donations, and other funding sources. These include:

- **Entrance fees and amenity fees.** The Federal Lands Recreation Enhancement Act (FLREA)[11] authorizes the Park Service to collect and use recreation fees, including entrance fees and amenity fees for certain equipment and services, such as campgrounds.
- **Franchise fees and commercial use authorization fees.** The National Park Service Concessions Management Improvement Act of 1998 (Concessions Act) authorizes the Park Service to collect and use certain fees from concessioners that operate businesses in park units.[12] Specifically, the Park Service may collect and use franchise fees from concessioners who operate restaurants, lodges, and other business operations inside park units. These fees are generally assessed as a percentage of the concessioners' total gross receipts. The Park Service also collects fees for commercial use authorizations, which include small-scale commercial activities, such as leading workshops or tours.
- **Rents.** The Park Service is authorized to collect and use certain rents.[13] Through its leasing program, the Park Service leases buildings and associated property to businesses, individuals, and government entities.

- **Donations.** The Park Service is authorized by law to receive and use cash donations and in-kind donations from individuals, nonprofit organizations, and corporations.[14] Examples of in-kind donations include artifacts or services provided by nonprofit partner groups on behalf of the Park Service. The Park Service is also authorized to develop agreements with nonprofit partner groups, known as friends groups and cooperating associations.[15] In general, friends groups engage in fundraising efforts on behalf of individual parks units, while cooperating associations provide interpretive services for visitors and manage retail operations at parks and share a portion of their proceeds from these operations with park units.[16] The Park Service also has a volunteer program authorized by the Volunteers in the Parks Act of 1969.[17] Volunteers help with a variety of tasks at park units, including doing maintenance work and providing interpretive services to visitors.
- Other funding sources. Other funding sources include transportation fees the Park Service collects to operate public transportation systems in park units; rents collected for employee housing; and funding from the U.S. Department of the Treasury for certain pension payments for United States Park Police annuitants.[18]

## Park Service's Total Funding Did Not Keep Pace with Inflation for Fiscal Years 2005 through 2014, Even with Increases in Fees and Donations

According to our analysis of OMB MAX data, total funding for the Park Service increased in nominal dollars from $2.7 billion in fiscal year 2005 to $3.1 billion in fiscal year 2014 (15 percent), as shown in table 1. However, when adjusted for inflation, total funding for the Park Service declined by 3 percent during this period.

For fiscal years 2005 through 2014, the largest component of funding for the Park Service was its annual appropriations, which comprised 88 percent of its total funding on average, with fees, donations, and other funding sources comprising the remaining 12 percent. Over time, there has been some growth in the proportion of total Park Service funding that fees, donations, and other funding sources comprise (see Figure. 1).

**Table 1. Total Funding for the National Park Service, Fiscal Year 2005 through Fiscal Year 2014 in Nominal Terms**

| Dollars in millions | | | | | | | | | | | |
|---|---|---|---|---|---|---|---|---|---|---|---|
| **Funding source** | **FY 05** | **FY 06** | **FY 07** | **FY 08** | **FY 09** | **FY 10** | **FY 11** | **FY 12** | **FY 13** | **FY 14** | **Change FY 05 – FY 14** |
| Annual appropriations[a] | $2,391 | $2,346 | $2,330 | $2,480 | $3,308 | $2,770 | $2,641 | $2,594 | $2,816 | $2,604 | 9% |
| Fees, donations, and other funding sources[b] | 288 | 310 | 333 | 377 | 358 | 381 | 364 | 410 | 394 | 473 | 64% |
| **Total** | **$2,679** | **$2,656** | **$2,663** | **$2,857** | **$3,666** | **$3,151** | **$3,005** | **$3,004** | **$3,210** | **$3,077** | **15%** |

Legend: FY = fiscal year.

Source: GAO analysis of Office of Management and Budget MAX data. | GAO-16-166

[a] This represents funding received through annual appropriations acts.

[b] This represents funding from fees, donations, and other sources. This includes recreation fees, commercial service fees, and philanthropic donations that the Park Service is authorized to collect and use.

Annual appropriations increased by 9 percent overall from fiscal year 2005 through fiscal year 2014 in nominal terms but declined by 8 percent after adjusting for inflation (see Figure 2). A large increase in appropriations came in fiscal year 2009, when the American Recovery and Reinvestment Act provided an additional $750 million to the Park Service.[19] Since fiscal year 2010, annual appropriations for the Park Service have generally declined. Park Service officials told us that flat or declining appropriations have made it difficult to cover increases in salary and expenses for agency employees and to address the agency's growing maintenance backlog. In addition, the number of park units in the system has been growing, and some Park Service officials said that this increase in units meant that the agency's appropriations had to be divided among an increasing number of units. In 2006, there were 390 park units, and there are 409 park units as of November 2015.

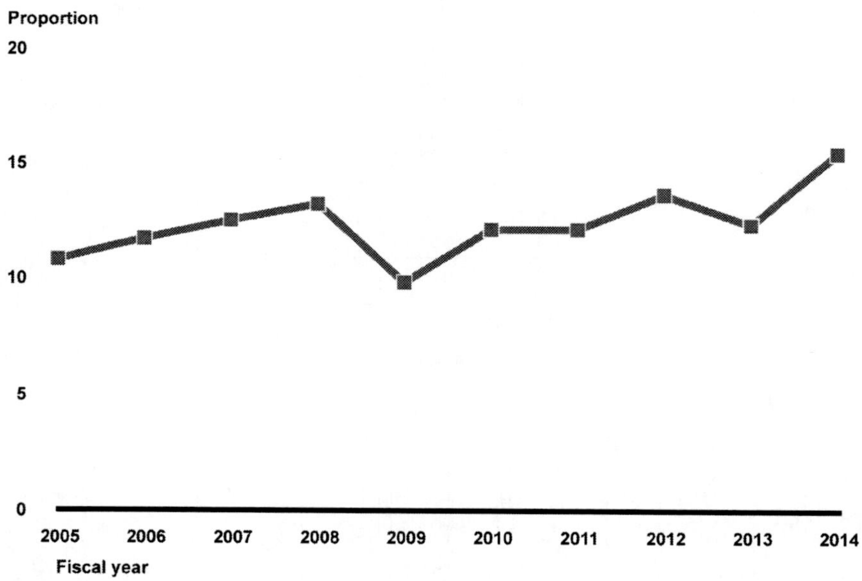


Source: GAO analysis of office of Management and Budget MAX Information System data. | GAO-16-166.

Note: This figure represents the proportion of Park Service's total funding that comes from fees, donations, and other sources. This includes recreation fees, commercial service fees, and philanthropic donations that the Park Service is authorized to collect.

Figure 1. Proportion of the National Park Service's Total Funding Comprised of Fees, Donations, and Other Funding Sources, Fiscal Year 2005 through Fiscal Year 2014.

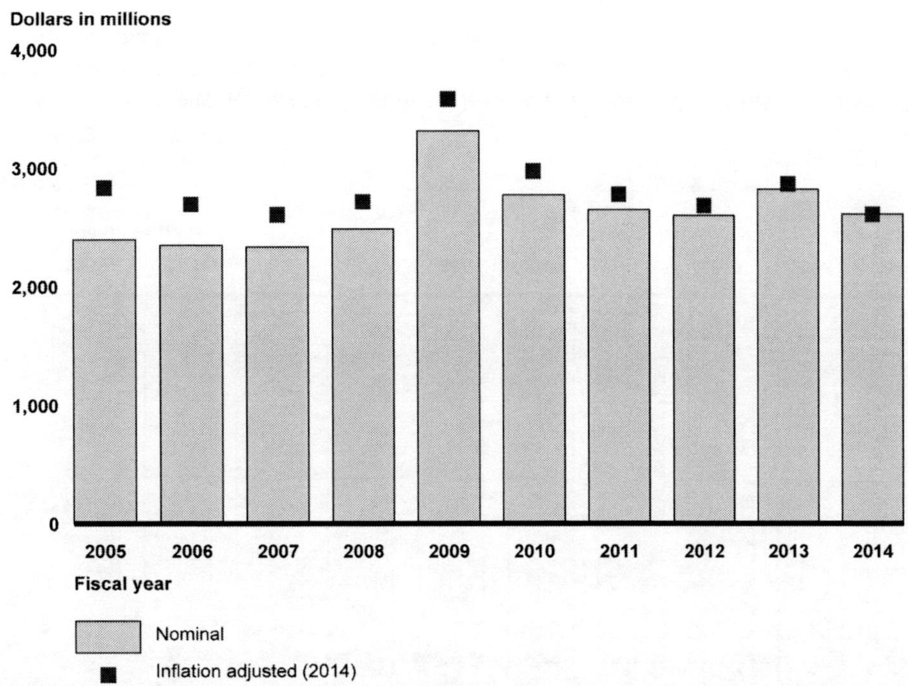


Source: GAO analysis of office of Management and Budget MAX Information System data. | GAO-16-166.

Note: A large increase in appropriations came in fiscal year 2009, when the American Recovery and Reinvestment Act provided an additional $750 million to the Park Service.

Figure 2. Annual Appropriations for the National Park Service, Fiscal Year 2005 through Fiscal Year 2014.

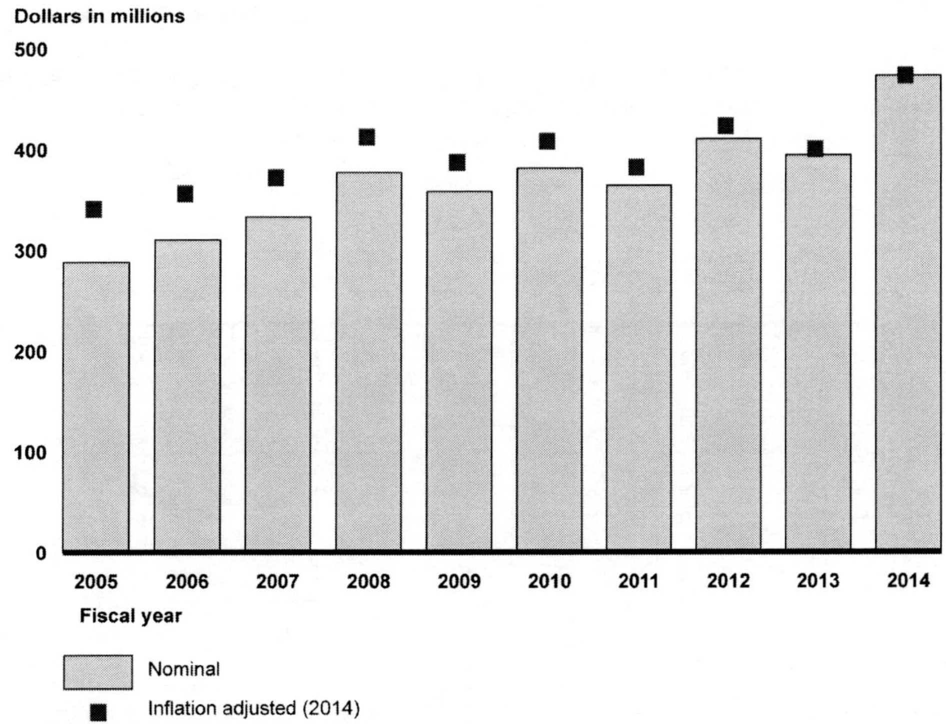


Source: GAO analysis of office of Management and Budget MAX Information System data. | GAO-16-166

Note: This figure represents funding from fees, donations, and other sources. This includes recreation fees, commercial service fees, and philanthropic donations that the Park Service is authorized to collect.

Figure 3. Fees, Donations, and Other Funding Sources for the Park Service, Fiscal Year 2005 through Fiscal Year 2014.

Fees, donations, and other funding sources grew 64 percent in nominal terms from fiscal year 2005 through fiscal year 2014 and have increased in most years, as shown in figure 3. Even after adjusting for inflation, funding from these sources increased by 39 percent during this period.

Recreation fees, commercial service fees, and cash donations comprised on average 74 percent of the total fees, donations, and other funding sources for the Park Service for fiscal years 2005 through 2014.[20] Park Service officials told us that these three revenue sources provided important support to park units. For example, from 2005 through 2011, recreation fees funded an estimated 8,575 projects at park units, including maintenance and other projects that enhanced the visitor experience, according to a 2012 report on the implementation of FLREA.[21] In addition, during that time period, the Park Service used revenue from franchise fees to reimburse numerous concessioners that improved facilities in park units. Further, philanthropic donations enabled some parks to complete projects, such as improving trails or rehabilitating visitor centers. Some Park Service officials voiced concern to us that fees and donations could be viewed as a substitute for annual appropriations. They said that these sources are to be viewed as a supplement to annual appropriations but not a replacement.

# Park Service's Revenues from Fees and Donations Increased to Varying Degrees from Fiscal Year 2005 through Fiscal Year 2014

Revenues from recreation and commercial service fees and donations from philanthropic sources grew from fiscal year 2005 through fiscal year 2014. Specifically, revenues from recreation fees increased 26 percent during the period, while revenue from commercial service fees nearly tripled. Meanwhile, cash donations from philanthropic sources have fluctuated, while volunteer support has consistently increased.

## Revenues from Recreation Fees Grew 26 Percent, and a Small Number of Parks Account for a Large Proportion of These Fees

According to our analysis of Park Service data, revenues from recreation fees increased from about $148 million to about $186 million (26 percent) during the period we examined, as shown in figure 4. With the exception of fiscal years 2009, 2010, and 2013, revenues from recreation fees increased over the prior year.

Revenues from recreation fees are comprised largely of entrance fees and amenity fees for equipment, services, and facilities, such as campsites. Revenues from entrance fees have been higher than amenity fees from fiscal year 2005 through fiscal year 2014, accounting for about 77 percent on average of the total recreation fees collected, with amenity fees on average accounting for the remaining 23 percent.[22]

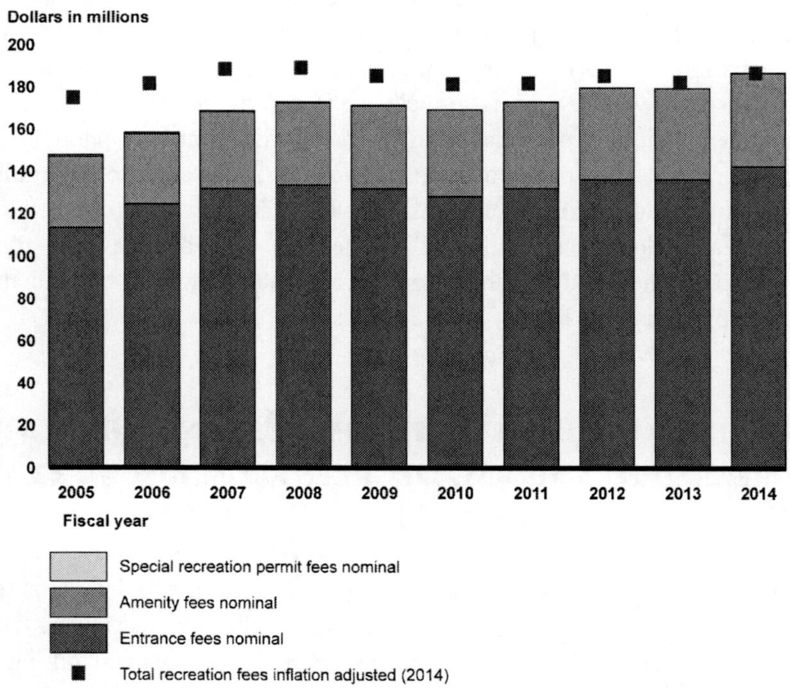


Source: GAO analysis of National Park Service data. | GAO-16-166

Note: Recreation fees include entrance, amenity, and special recreation permits collected by park units. Special recreation permit fees accounted on average for about 0.22 percent of total recreation fees during the period we examined. Amenity fees are for equipment, services, and facilities such as campsites, while special recreation permits are for specialized recreation activities such as motorized recreational vehicle use.

Figure 4. Total Recreation Fees Collected by the National Park Service, Fiscal Year 2005 through Fiscal Year 2014.

Although recreation fee revenues have been generally increasing, the number of park units collecting entrance fees has declined from fiscal year 2008, the first year for which data are available according to Park Service officials, through fiscal year 2015. The number of park units charging amenity fees has remained largely constant over this period (see table 2).

The decision to charge recreation fees involves individual park units, which make proposals to charge fees, and regional and headquarters officials who approve these fees. According to Park Service guidance, one of the guiding principles of the program is that parks will not collect recreation fees if the cost of collection exceeds the amount of revenue generated.[23] For example, some park units do not have many visitors, so the administrative costs of charging these fees, which include paying staff to collect them, purchasing cash registers to process them, and hiring an armored car service to deposit them, can outweigh the anticipated revenues.

Even with the decline in the number of parks collecting recreation fees, revenues grew over the period we examined, largely because the fees collected at a small number of parks account for a large portion of the fees collected. In fiscal year 2014, five national parks—Grand Canyon, Yosemite, Yellowstone, Rocky Mountain, and Zion—accounted for $59.6 million or about one-third of the total recreation fees collected that year. In addition, according to our analysis of the Park Service data, the top 50 park units collected about 88 percent of the total recreation fees collected in fiscal year 2014.

**Table 2. Number of Park Service Units Charging Recreation Fees, Fiscal Year 2008 through Fiscal Year 2015**

| Fiscal year | Park units collecting entrance fees[a] | Park units collecting amenity fees[b] | Park units collecting both entrance fees and amenity fees |
|---|---|---|---|
| 2008 | 147 | 132 | 87 |
| 2009 | 143 | 132 | 86 |
| 2010 | 140 | 131 | 86 |
| 2011 | 134 | 131 | 86 |
| 2012 | 133 | 132 | 86 |
| 2013 | 131 | 131 | 84 |
| 2014 | 130 | 131 | 83 |
| 2015 | 128 | 130 | 82 |

Source: GAO analysis of National Park Service data. | GAO-16-166

[a] Entrance fees are paid by visitors to enter a park unit for a certain period of time.

[b] Amenity fees are paid by visitors for equipment, services, and facilities, such as campsites.

## TOP 10 PARK UNITS IN RECREATION FEES COLLECTED, FISCAL YEAR 2014

Dollars in thousands

| Park unit name | Recreation fees collected |
|---|---|
| Grand Canyon National Park | $19,051 |
| Yosemite National Park | 18,790 |
| Yellowstone National Park | 9,449 |
| Zion National Park | 6,487 |
| Rocky Mountain National Park | 5,804 |
| Lake Mead National Recreation Area | 4,593 |
| Shenandoah National Park | 4,572 |
| Sequoia National Park and Kings Canyon National Park[a] | 4,564 |
| Grand Teton National Park | 4,330 |
| Glacier National Park | $4,113 |

Source: GAO analysis of National Park Service data. | GAO-16-166

[a] Recreation fees are collected jointly for Kings Canyon and Sequoia National Parks. Specifically, entrance fees allow access to both parks.

## Revenues from Commercial Service Fees and Rents Almost Tripled, and Concessions Contracts Generate the Majority of These Revenues

According to our analysis of Park Service data, revenues from commercial service fees and rents almost tripled during the period, growing from almost $33 million in fiscal year 2005 to about $95 million in fiscal year 2014, as shown in Figure 5.[24] Revenues from franchise fees, rents,[25] and commercial use authorization fees all grew during this period. Specifically, revenues from franchise fees almost tripled, growing from about $29 million in fiscal year 2005 to about $85 million in fiscal year 2014. In addition, rents grew from about $2 million in fiscal year 2005 to almost $8 million in fiscal year 2014, and fees from commercial use authorizations more than doubled from about $988,000 in fiscal year 2005 to about $2 million in fiscal year 2014.

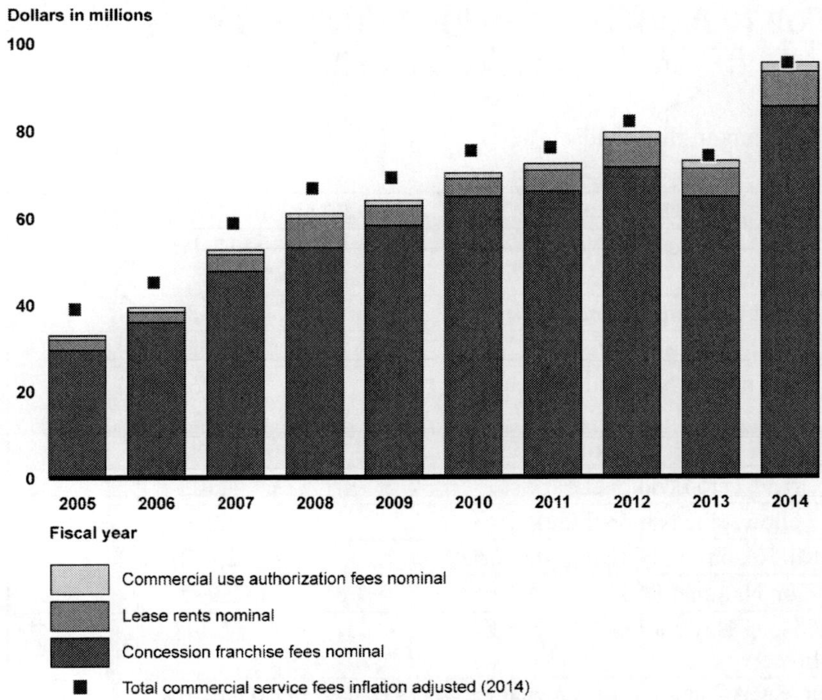


Source: GAO analysis of National Park Service data. | GAO-16-166

Note: Commercial service fees are comprised of franchise fees paid by concessioners who operate businesses in park units, rents received from individuals, businesses or governmental entities leasing Park Service buildings, and fees paid for commercial use authorizations, which include small-scale commercial activities.

Figure 5. Commercial Service Revenues Collected by the National Park Service by Type, Fiscal Year 2005 through Fiscal Year 2014.

The Park Service generates the vast majority of its commercial service revenues from franchise fees associated with concession contracts. Specifically, these fees accounted for about 90 percent of all commercial service revenues in fiscal year 2014. A small number of large concessions contracts accounted for the majority of these fees. According to Park Service officials, data from concessioners' 2014 annual financial reports showed that 51 of the agency's approximately 500 concessions contracts generated 84 percent of all franchise fees paid to the Park Service in fiscal year 2014. Leases generated about 8 percent of fiscal year 2014 commercial service revenues, and commercial use authorizations generated about 2 percent.

## TOP 10 PARK UNITS IN FRANCHISE FEES COLLECTED, FISCAL YEAR 2014

Dollars in thousands

| Park unit name | Franchise fees collected |
|---|---|
| Statue of Liberty National Monument | $17,445 |
| Grand Canyon National Park | 11,428 |
| Yosemite National Park | 10,974 |
| Golden Gate National Recreation Area | 8,220 |
| Denali National Park and Preserve | 4,812 |
| Grand Teton National Park | 4,303 |
| Yellowstone National Park | 4,259 |
| Mt. Rushmore National Memorial | 2,858 |
| Zion National Park | 2,732 |
| Glacier Bay National Park and Preserve | $2,398 |

Source: GAO analysis of National Park Service data. | GAO-16-166

The growth in commercial service revenues can be attributed in part to an increase in the franchise fee rates that concessioners are paying to the Park Service. According to Park Service officials, franchise fees for individual contracts have increased an average of 2.4 percentage points as they have turned over and been awarded under the terms of the new Concessions Act. In addition, our analysis of Park Service data showed that the number of park units collecting commercial service fees has grown.[26] In fiscal year 2005, 146 parks reported collecting at least one type of commercial service fee; the number grew to 176 by 2014. According to Park Service officials, growth in commercial service revenues can also be attributed to improved economic conditions, which has led to increased visitation levels at park units and higher gross receipts for concessioners.

## Cash Donations to the Park Service Fluctuated, and Volunteer Support Consistently Increased

Cash donations to the Park Service did not have a discernible trend from fiscal year 2005 through fiscal year 2014, and there was considerable fluctuation in donations during this period (see Figure 6), ranging from $19.5 million in fiscal year 2011 to $94.7 million in fiscal year 2014. According to a senior Park Service official, this variation is largely due to donors contributing to large projects at particular park units that attracted the attention of donors in certain years. For example, $65.5 million of the $94.7 in total cash donations (69 percent) the Park Service received in fiscal year 2014 is from donations to renovate the museum and build a new visitor's center at the Gateway Arch in St. Louis, which is part of the Jefferson National Expansion Memorial. Park Service officials also pointed out that economic factors play a role in influencing donation trends, noting that donations declined after the 2008 U.S. recession.

### TOP 10 PARK UNITS IN CASH DONATIONS, FISCAL YEAR 2014

Dollars in thousands

| Park unit name | Donations received |
|---|---|
| Jefferson National Expansion Memorial | $65,456 |
| Flight 93 National Memorial | 3,200 |
| Yosemite National Park | 2,857 |
| Great Smoky Mountains National Park | 2,690 |
| Yellowstone National Park | 2,082 |
| Grand Teton National Park | 1,341 |
| Grand Canyon National Park | 1,159 |
| Golden Gate National Recreation Area | 1,144 |
| Indiana Dunes National Lakeshore | 815 |
| Gettysburg National Military Park | $663 |

Source: GAO analysis of National Park Service data. | GAO-16-166

Cash donations to the Park Service come from a variety of sources, including friends groups and cooperating associations. These groups also provide in-kind donations to the Park Service, which include artifacts donated or services provided to the agency. In general, we found that total donations from friends groups—both cash and in-kind donations—rose from about $68 million in fiscal year 2005 to about $147 million in 2011, the latest year for which data are available according to Park Service officials. Regarding donations from cooperating associations, Park Service officials and cooperating association officials told us that donations have generally been increasing, although this trend has been tempered by declining book sales nationwide, which have traditionally been a key source of cooperating associations' revenues at the stores they operate.

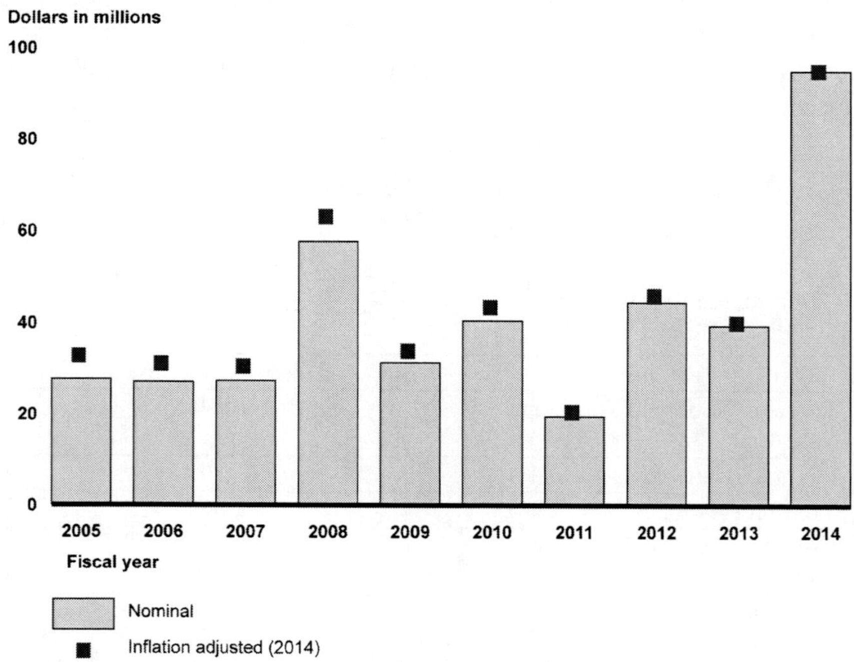


Source: GAO analysis of National Park Service data. | GAO-16-166

Note: $65.5 million of the $94.7 in total cash donations (69 percent) the Park Service received in fiscal year 2014 is from donations to renovate the museum and build a new visitor's center at the Gateway Arch in St. Louis, which is part of the Jefferson National Expansion Memorial.

Figure 6. Cash Donations to the National Park Service, Fiscal Year 2005 through Fiscal Year 2014.

**Table 3. Park Service's Entrance Fee Schedule for 2006 and 2014**

| | Annual pass | | Per vehicle | | Per person | | Per motorcycle | |
|---|---|---|---|---|---|---|---|---|
| | 2006 | 2014 | 2006 | 2014 | 2006 | 2014 | 2006 | 2014 |
| **Group 1:** | | | | | | | | |
| National historic sites, military parks, battlefields, battlefield parks, preserves, memorials/shrines, and parkways | $20 | $30 | $10 | $15 | $5 | $7 | $5 | $10 |
| **Group 2:** | | | | | | | | |
| National seashores, recreation areas, monuments, lakeshores, and historical parks | $30 | $40 | $15 | $20 | $7 | $10 | $10 | $15 |
| **Group 3:** | | | | | | | | |
| National parks | $40 | $50 | $20 | $25 | $10 | $12 | $15 | $20 |
| **Group 4:** | | | | | | | | |
| National parks[a] | $50 | $60 | $25 | $30 | $12 | $15 | $20 | $25 |

Source: National Park Service. | GAO-16-166

[a] Group 4 national parks may charge higher entrance fees than group 3 national parks. The following 10 national parks are Group 4 national parks: Bryce Canyon, Glacier, Grand Canyon, Grand Teton, Rocky Mountain, Sequoia, Kings Canyon, Yellowstone, Yosemite, and Zion.

According to Park Service data, volunteer support for the agency has increased steadily. Specifically, the number of volunteers increased from about 132,000 in fiscal year 2005 to about 248,000 in fiscal year 2014, and the estimated cash value of their work increased from about $93 million to about $155 million during this period.[27] The number of volunteers increased every year, except for fiscal year 2013. According to a senior Park Service official, the decline in the number of volunteers that year was attributable to Hurricane Sandy and the 2013 federal government shutdown, both of which disrupted the typical operations of the Park Service.[28]

# PARK SERVICE HAS INITIATIVES UNDER WAY TO INCREASE REVENUES FROM FEES AND DONATIONS, BUT CERTAIN FACTORS COMPLICATE THESE EFFORTS

The Park Service has efforts under way to increase revenues from recreation and commercial service fees along with philanthropic donations. However, certain factors complicate these efforts and limit the agency's ability to increase revenue from these sources.

## Park Service Recently Increased Recreation Fees at Many Parks, but Faces Challenges to Further Increases

In 2014, the Park Service encouraged park units that were collecting recreation fees to increase them, and 111 park units subsequently elected to do so, as of September 2015. Park Service officials told us that parks are expected to examine their amenity fees each year; however, there are no plans to regularly reassess entrance fees. The Park Service's ability to increase funding from recreation fees is also limited by legislation and park-specific characteristics.

## Park Service Increased Both Entrance and Amenity Fees at Several Parks but Does Not Plan to Regularly Reassess Entrance Fees

The Park Service has recently increased entrance and amenity fees at several parks. In August 2014, the Director of the Park Service issued a memorandum that ended a moratorium on entrance fee increases that had been in place since 2008 and updated the agency's entrance fee rate schedule for the first time since 2006 (see table 3).[29] Like the 2006 fee schedule, the updated schedule separates the park units that collect entrance fees into four groups by type of park unit. If adopted, these fees represent an increase of 20 to 50 percent in most instances over the 2006 fee schedule, depending on the type of park unit and type of entrance fee being charged. Park Service officials told us that the agency estimates that $58 million in additional entrance fees could be generated if all parks charging entrance fees followed the schedule and visitation is not impacted by the increase in fees.

The Park Service gave discretion to the park units to decide whether to increase entrance fees, and the memo states "if there is significant public controversy, a park may choose not to implement new fees, may phase in the new rates over three years, or delay the new rates until 2016 or 2017." To assess public reaction to proposed fee changes, the memorandum encouraged park units to conduct public outreach in late summer or fall of 2014. According to Park Service officials we interviewed, park units used different methods to conduct this outreach, including using social media, holding public meetings, and meeting with congressional delegations.

According to the memorandum, once public outreach was complete, each park unit that chose to proceed with a rate change had to submit their proposed change to regional and headquarters offices for approval. Of the 130 park units that charged an entrance fee in 2014, 92 park units proposed increasing the per person entrance fee, and 60 park units proposed increasing the per vehicle entrance fee, and all of them received approval to do so.[30] For those increasing fees, a number of park units chose to charge less than the revised entrance fee schedule by 2017. Specifically, of the 92 park units that received approval to increase fees for individuals, 59 (64 percent) will be charging an entrance fee for individuals in line with the proposed schedule; the remainder elected to charge less than what the schedule recommends.

A senior Park Service official told us that discretion was given to the parks under agency guidance about whether to follow the fee schedule, and fee increases needed to be supported by the public. According to the memorandum establishing the new entrance fee schedule, "the goal (if supported by civic engagement) is for all entrance fee parks to align with the standard rate for their group by 2017." However, several park units that are collecting some type of entrance fee in 2015 did not increase entrance fees, and may not align with the fee schedule by 2017, unless they undertake efforts to do so. In addition, Park Service does not require park units to provide information supporting their decisions on not increasing entrance fee rates or increasing their fees by less than the fee schedule. According to a senior Park Service official, providing this information was not required because it was not compulsory that park units increase their fees. However, *Federal Internal Control Standards* state that for an agency to run its operations, it must have reliable and timely communication and that information is needed throughout the agency to achieve its objectives.[31] By not requiring that parks provide information on decisions that deviate from the fee schedule, the Park Service may not have relevant information that would help to manage changes to recreation fees more effectively and ensure that park units are taking steps to determine whether entrance fees are set at a reasonable level.

Regarding amenity fees, the August 2014 Park Service Director's memorandum encouraged park units that charge amenity fees to examine them to determine whether they should increase. In order to increase these fees, the memorandum directs park units to conduct studies to compare the amenities offered in their parks and associated fees with those offered by private businesses in the surrounding area. Of the 131 park units that charged amenity fees in 2014, 55 park units received approval from Park Service headquarters to increase their amenity fees. Many of these parks received headquarters approval to increase fees at campgrounds. For example, Whiskeytown National Recreation Area in California received approval to increase fees $5 a night in most cases for recreation vehicle, tent, and horse camping. In general, Park Service officials told us that they expect parks to conduct comparability studies on an annual basis to see if amenity fees should be raised as part of the annual process to request changing fees, which is laid out in Park Service guidance.[32]

Unlike amenity fees, Park Service officials told us there were no plans to periodically review entrance fees to see if they should be increased. Our 2008 guide on federal user fees states that if federal user fees are not reviewed and adjusted regularly, federal agencies run the risk of undercharging or overcharging users.[33] Moreover, Park Service guidance directs the agency to ensure its fees are set at a reasonable level, but this guidance does not direct that these fees be periodically reviewed.[34] In a 2015 report, the Department of the Interior Inspector General recommended that the Park Service establish intervals for periodic reviews of its entrance fees to ensure that the fee schedule remains up to date.[35] Park Service officials told us they were hesitant to commit to such reviews until FLREA is reauthorized because they were unsure if they would continue to have the authority to continue charging entrance fees.[36] However, Park Service has not required periodic reviews of entrance fees for the 11 years that FLREA has been in place.[37] By not regularly reviewing its entrance fee schedule, the Park Service is missing an opportunity to ensure that these fees are reasonable.

### *Legislation and Park-Specific Characteristics Limit Recreation Fee Collection*

The Park Service's ability to further increase revenues from recreation fees is limited by legislation and park-specific characteristics.

**Legislation.** According to Park Service data, 58 park units are prohibited by law from charging entrance fees. For example, the Alaska National Interest Lands Conservation Act prohibits the Park Service from charging entrance fees at all park units in Alaska.[38] FLREA prohibits the Park Service from charging entrance fees at parks that lie within the District of Columbia,[39] and the National Parks and Recreation Act of 1978 prohibits the Park Service from charging entrance fees at Point Reyes National Seashore.[40] Park Service officials also said there were limits to how much the agency could raise fees because FLREA requires that the agency consider the impacts of fees on visitors, and the Park Service did not want to dissuade visitors from coming to parks. For example, there was opposition from the public to implementing entrance fees at additional areas of the Chesapeake and Ohio (C&O) National Historical Park and, in response, park officials withdrew this proposal in February 2015.[41]

FLREA also directed the Secretary of the Interior to establish an interagency pass that covers entrance fees and certain amenity fees for all federal recreational lands. The price of the pass is $80 annually, as of October 2015, and covers national park units, as well as recreational lands managed by U.S. Forest Service, Bureau of Reclamation, Bureau of Land Management, and the U.S. Fish and Wildlife Service. However, FLREA limits agencies' ability to increase revenue from recreation fees.[42] For example, the law prohibits charging entrance fees to persons under 16 years of age. FLREA also requires the Secretary of the Interior to offer a lifetime interagency pass for a one-time $10 price to senior citizens, defined as being over 62 years of age, and requires that free interagency passes be made available to permanently disabled people.

While under FLREA, the price of the annual interagency pass can be changed by the agencies that administer it, the law does not provide this flexibility for the $10 lifetime senior pass, the free annual pass for disabled individuals, or free entry for those under age 16. Interior's Inspector General found that this aspect of FLREA "hampers agencies' flexibility and their ability to make business decisions" and concluded that free and substantially discounted passes represent missed opportunities for revenue.[43] The price of the senior pass has been $10 since 1993, but a bill introduced in September 2015 would increase this price to a one- time amount matching the price of the annual interagency pass, which is $80, as of October 2015.[44] If this occurred, it could generate about another $35 million in revenue annually, assuming that the same number of passes was sold, as in fiscal year 2014, which was about 500,000.[45] Because of the limitations in FLREA, Park Service and the other agencies that administer the recreation fee program do not have the flexibility to periodically reassess and change the price of the lifetime senior pass. Providing this flexibility to these agencies would allow them to consider adjusting fees periodically, which is consistent with our guide on federal user fees.[46]

**Park-specific characteristics.** At some park units, collecting recreation fees is precluded by the configuration of the parks or is not economically advantageous. For example, some park units have many entry points, which make the logistics of collecting entrance fees difficult, according to Park Service officials. In addition, as previously described, at some park units, it may not be economically advantageous to collect recreation fees at some park units. For example, at parks with few visitors, the costs of administering the fee collection program would be a significant portion of the total fees collected, and these parks may not choose to charge an entrance fee. Other park units—for example, national historic sites—may not offer amenities, such as campsites, for which the Park Service could charge fees.

## Park Service Increased Revenues from Commercial Services and Is Looking for New Opportunities to Generate Revenue, but Several Factors Complicate These Efforts

The Park Service increased revenues from commercial service fees from fiscal year 2005 through 2014, in part by increasing the franchise fees that concessioners are to pay and by taking steps to make certain contracts more attractive to potential bidders. However, several factors complicate these efforts.

### Park Service Increased Concessions Revenues and Is Looking for Opportunities to Increase Revenues from Other Commercial Services

The Park Service increased revenues from commercial service fees from fiscal year 2005 through fiscal year 2014, in part by increasing the minimum franchise fees included in contract prospectuses. According to Park Service officials, the agency increased the minimum franchise fee by modifying the process they used to develop contract prospectuses, which describe the services concessioners are to provide, any investments required for the operation, such as maintenance or equipment, and the minimum franchise fee, among other things. After a prospectus is issued, potential concessioners submit bids that include, among other things, the franchise fee they agree to pay if they are awarded the contract—which has to be equal to or higher than the minimum in the prospectus—along with details about the services they propose to provide. Before 1998, when the Concessions Act was enacted, the Park Service set minimum franchise fees based on limited financial reviews of concessioners' financial statements, according to Park Service officials. After 1998, Park Service officials told us that they started hiring hospitality consultants to help them with the financial aspects of contract prospectuses to meet the requirements of the new act. Specifically, the agency started working with hospitality consultants to conduct in-depth financial analyses to develop minimum franchise fees for the Park Service's largest contracts—those with gross revenues above $5 million. These analyses involve estimating concessioners' costs and anticipated revenues and comparing the estimated profitability of the concessions operations with industry standards. Park Service officials and hospitality consultants told us that these more sophisticated analyses allowed the agency to better estimate the franchise fees that concessioners could pay while still having a reasonable opportunity for profit, as required by the Concessions Act, which led to higher franchise fees.[47]

Park Service officials also made efforts to increase revenues from commercial service fees by working to make concessions contracts more attractive and increasing competition among potential bidders. Park Service officials told us that increased competition among potential concessioners generally results in higher franchise fees in winning contracts. Our analysis of Park Service data also found that increased competition was associated with higher franchise fees. Specifically, based on our analysis of 25 large contracts awarded between fiscal years 2005 and 2014 we found that the Park Service earned an average of 5 percent in franchise fees from contracts that attracted 1 or 2 bidders and an average of 16 percent in franchise fees from contracts that attracted 3 or more bidders.[48] One of the ways that Park Service officials said they tried to make concessions contracts attractive to more potential bidders was by reducing the amount of Leaseholder Surrender Interest (LSI) that had accumulated under certain contracts. LSI generally represents the depreciated value of capital improvements made by a concessioner to a property, such as building a new structure or completing a major rehabilitation.[49] If a contract is awarded to a different concessioner when the contract ends, the Concessions Act requires the previous concessioner to be reimbursed for any LSI. The previous concessioner may be reimbursed by the new contract holder or the Park Service. Park Service officials and concessioners we spoke with said that LSI can create barriers to competition because few companies have the resources to reimburse the previous concessioner. Park Service officials told us that they chose to reduce the LSI associated with certain contracts because these contracts would otherwise have attracted few bidders. For example, in 2014, the Park Service spent almost $100 million reducing LSI to increase competition for a large concessions contract at Grand Canyon National Park. The Park Service initially invested $19 million in LSI payments. However, even with this reduction in LSI, the Park Service did not receive offers that met the terms of its first three prospectuses, and agency officials said that the level of LSI remained a barrier to potential bidders. As a result, the Park Service paid an additional $81 million to further reduce LSI. The Park Service received multiple bids on the fourth prospectus for this contract. Park Service officials told us that they plan to award this contract by January 1, 2016.

In addition to reducing LSI associated with certain contracts, the Park Service has limited the amount of LSI that potential bidders can incur in new contracts, according to Park Service and concessioner officials we spoke with. Park Service officials told us that limiting LSI could reduce start-up costs associated with future contracts since new concessioners would not have to reimburse previous concessioners for accumulated LSI. However, some concessioners told us that limiting LSI could lead to lower levels of investment in concessioner-run properties, since concessioners may be less likely to make capital improvements if they are not reimbursed for these investments. This, in turn, could contribute to additional asset degradation and increased future maintenance costs, according to some concessioners we spoke with.

Park Service officials also have looked for opportunities to increase revenues from leases and commercial use authorizations. Specifically, the Park Service hired a national leasing manager in 2015 to formalize its leasing program, and some parks units and regions have developed active leasing programs. For example, from 2009 through 2014, the Northeast region increased the number of leases from 25 to 76. As a result, the region more than doubled the revenue it generated from rents and payments made in lieu of rent,[50] which increased from almost $14 million to $38 million during this time period. According to regional Park Service officials, the region increased its leases by increasing the number of full-time leasing positions and by hiring staff with real estate expertise to help advise parks on developing leases and perform market studies to set rental rates.

The Park Service also has developed a new policy that has the potential to increase revenues from commercial use authorizations, according to Park Service officials. Traditionally, fees for commercial use authorizations were set to recover costs that park officials incurred administering the program. According to several park unit officials we spoke with, these fees ranged from $100 to $350 per permit. In 2015, the Park Service developed guidance that allows park officials to charge businesses a fee based on a percentage of gross receipts or a fee that is sufficient to cover administrative and management costs incurred issuing these commercial use authorizations—whichever is more. For example, the new guidance allows park officials to charge recreation service providers that generate less than $250,000 in annual gross receipts the greater of either 3 percent of gross receipts or $500. Some businesses operating under commercial use authorizations generate significant revenues, sometimes hundreds of thousands of dollars, according to Park Service officials. As a result, officials said that this shift has the potential to increase revenues because the resulting fees would be higher than the flat fees that have traditionally been charged.

### *Several Factors Complicate Park Service's Efforts to Increase Revenues from Commercial Service Fees*

Several factors complicate the Park Service's efforts to increase revenues from commercial service fees. In particular, officials noted that the Park Service is required by law to balance a number of priorities. Specifically, under the Concessions Act, accommodations, facilities, and services offered under a concessions contract must be consistent to the highest practicable degree with the preservation and conservation of park units they are proposed to operate in, provide a reasonable opportunity for profit to concessioners, and offer reasonable rates for facilities and services to the public. The law does not require the Park Service to maximize franchise fees; instead, it states that franchise fees are a lower priority than protecting, conserving and preserving park units or providing necessary and appropriate facilities and services to visitors at reasonable rates. As a result, Park Service officials told us that increasing revenues from franchise fees can be challenging.

The Park Service's efforts to increase revenues from commercial service fees also have been affected by limited competition for some concessions contracts. Our analysis of Park Service data found that 32 percent (8 of 25) of the Park Service's largest contracts—those generating $5 million or more—awarded between fiscal years 2005 and 2014 attracted one bidder. These 25 contracts generated about 45 percent of the $65 million in franchise fees collected by the Park Service in fiscal year 2013, the most recent year for which data are available. Park Service officials told us that, of these 25 contracts, 2 contracts for lodging services initially received no bids. In addition, some parks offer limited opportunities for revenue generation, which may in turn limit the number of bidders. For example, Park Service officials told us that some park units are located in remote locations that attract few visitors or have short tourist seasons, which limits the potential profitability of these contracts. According to Park Service officials, they are pleased to receive one bid in such cases.

Adjusting a concessions contract to provide additional services, which could increase revenues for concessioners and the Park Service, can be a lengthy process, according to some concessioners we spoke with. For example, one concessioner that provides transportation services at a park told us that his company proposed increasing the number of park visitors transported per day to levels consistent with the park's management plan. This proposed change took 20 months to be reviewed and approved by the Park Service, which, according to the concessioner, resulted in lost revenue for both the concessioner and Park Service. Another transportation concessioner told us about similar challenges adjusting his company's operating plan to increase service hours by 30 minutes. Although such a change in operating hours is generally the purview of the park superintendent, according to the concessioner, the change took 5 years to be approved due to turnover in park leadership and park budget constraints.

Park Service officials told us that they act as quickly as possible when they receive requests to change or increase concessioners' services but, in some cases, it takes time to collect and assess the necessary information to make an informed decision. For example, according to Park Service officials, the agency considers the impact of the proposed change on park operations and on other business operations in the park. Park Service officials also told us that they are developing guidance to establish factors to consider for adding services to help park unit staff when considering concessioners' requests. Proposed factors include whether the proposed services complement the terms of the current contract and whether there will be environmental impacts at the park unit from these services. In addition, concessioners must be fully compliant with their current contracts before requests to add services may be considered. As of August 2015, this guidance was under development, and agency officials were uncertain when it would be issued.

Efforts to increase revenues from leases and commercial use authorizations also face challenges. According to Park Service officials, leasing opportunities can be limited because some park units do not have buildings available to lease or the facilities they have are not suitable for leasing due to their poor physical condition. In addition, park officials at two parks we visited told us that they do not have sufficient staff to manage a leasing program. For commercial use authorizations, some park officials we spoke with said that changing their fee structure to one based on a percentage of business owners' gross revenues could pose a financial burden to smaller businesses that have low profit margins yet provide important services for park visitors. For example, park officials at one park told us that some businesses have held commercial use authorizations to deliver portable toilets, which they said is an essential service during large events. These officials told us that these businesses have relatively low profit margins and may be unwilling to operate in parks if they had to pay higher fees.

## Park Service Has Sought to Increase Philanthropic Donations, but Several Factors Limit Its Ability to Do So

To increase philanthropic donations, the Park Service is leveraging opportunities arising from its centennial anniversary in 2016, adjusting relevant policies, helping to increase the fundraising capacity of its nonprofit partners, and training its own staff on ways to collaborate more effectively with nonprofit partners. Several factors limiting the Park Service's ability to increase philanthropic support include attractiveness of certain projects needing donations, limited capacity to manage volunteers, and lack of detailed information on donations.

### *Park Service Is Leveraging Its Centennial Anniversary, Revising Policy, and Providing Other Assistance to Increase Donations*

To increase philanthropic donations, the Park Service is leveraging opportunities arising from its centennial anniversary in 2016. The Centennial Campaign has two primary efforts—fundraising and public outreach—both of which are being conducted in collaboration with the Park Service's congressionally chartered nonprofit partner, the National Park Foundation (Foundation).

- **Fundraising.** The Park Service and the Foundation have launched a major fundraising campaign, which aims to raise $250 million in donations by 2018. These funds will be used to support 100 projects that protect resources, connect visitors with the parks, and develop the next generation of park stewards. For example, in the area of protecting resources, projects include rehabilitating Constitution Gardens in Washington, D.C., and restoring an area of large Sequoia trees to a more natural state in Yosemite's Mariposa Grove.[51]

- **Public Outreach.** In collaboration with the Foundation, the Park Service launched the "Find Your Park" campaign in 2015. This public outreach effort is designed to encourage Americans to visit park units, generate interest in parks, and help raise financial and in-kind support for park units. This effort uses social media and disseminates marketing materials online and in park units. The Park Service has partnered on this campaign with certain major donors, which each made at least $500,000 in contributions to the Foundation to support the campaign. Figure 7 shows examples of posters developed for the campaign to be displayed in park units and also used in online and print advertising.

Source: National Park Service. | GAO-16-166

Figure 7. "Find Your Park" Campaign Materials.

The Park Service also has allocated about $49 million in funds appropriated by Congress for the centennial anniversary. Congress has also appropriated funds to be used for matching grants. Specifically, Congress appropriated $25 million in 2008, $15 million in 2010,[52] and $10 million in fiscal year 2015 to match philanthropic donations dollar-for- dollar to fund projects in park units. To be considered, proposed projects are to benefit one or more Park Service areas and have matching donations of at least 50 percent of project costs, according to the Park Service. Agency officials have prioritized projects with higher rates of matching donations, and considered the timeliness of donations, readiness of projects, and whether proposed projects address centennial and service-wide goals, such as high-priority deferred maintenance. Examples include rehabilitating the underground Franklin Court Museum at Independence National Historical Park and reconstructing roads, parking, walks, signs, and pedestrian areas to meet park road standards, accessibility standards, and historical context at Roosevelt Arch in Yellowstone National Park.

Since 2014, the Park Service has also been revising its policies related to philanthropy to help increase donations. Specifically, the Park Service has been revising *Director's Order 21*—the Park Service's main policy governing donations and fundraising. Some nonprofit partners told us that this guidance lengthened the donations process in the past by requiring significant Park Service review. Park Service documentation suggests that, when approved, the revised *Director's Order 21* will likely shift greater authority to regional directors and superintendents to accept donations and approve fundraising agreements. For example, current policy allows regional directors to approve donations less than $1 million. The revised policy, which will likely be signed in early 2016, may allow the Park Service Director to delegate approval authority to regional directors for donations up to $5 million. The Park Service is also revising *Director's Order 7*, which addresses volunteering, and *Reference Manual 32*, its internal guidance on cooperating associations and is planning to complete these revisions in late 2015. According to Park Service officials involved with these revisions, the goal of these revisions is to emphasize the importance of collaboration between Park Service and its partners.

In addition, in January 2015 the Park Service temporarily waived three parts of its policies to help with centennial fundraising efforts. First, Park Service policy generally prohibits naming park assets as a form of donor recognition. For example, buildings, vehicles, and park features are not to bear donor names. Park Service waived this policy with regard to certain donations for items including benches, bricks, motor vehicles, and rooms in buildings—although buildings themselves are still prohibited from bearing donors' names.[53] Second, Park Service policy generally prohibits donor recognition from including corporate logos in park units. The Park Service waived this policy to allow corporate logos to be included on vehicles under certain conditions. Figure 8 provides an example of a corporate logo displayed on a Park Service vehicle. Third, the Park Service also issued a waiver allowing it to advertise with an alcohol company. All three of these waivers will be effective until 2017, when Park Service will reevaluate them to determine if they should remain in place, according to a Park Service official.

The Park Service has also sought to increase philanthropic donations by encouraging the Foundation to expand and by helping friends groups increase their fundraising capacity. Specifically, the Park Service encouraged the Foundation to restructure and expand its staffing to better align with the current philanthropic practices. Since 2008, the Foundation has added 50 people and created three offices focused on corporate giving, private giving, and marketing. According to Foundation officials, the Foundation plans to continue increased fundraising efforts after the centennial campaign. With regard to friends groups, the Park Service has begun training its own staff on ways in which they can collaborate more effectively with nonprofit partners on their fundraising efforts. Park unit officials we spoke with told us that they help friends groups with their member outreach by attending fundraising events to describe the park's needs to potential donors. In addition, park unit officials work with friends groups to identify potential projects that need funds and that donors would likely support. Park Service officials told us that improving the fundraising capacity of friends groups is important since several new friends groups have been started in the past 10 years, and many have not yet developed fundraising skills.

The Park Service has also taken steps to increase volunteerism. Specifically, the Park Service allocated an additional $2 million in fiscal year 2015 to pay for 70 new volunteer coordinators, known as Centennial Volunteer Ambassadors. According to the Park Service, these 1-year internship positions will be dispersed throughout the Park Service. These coordinators will be responsible for helping to design and coordinate volunteer training and service. They will also perform outreach to attract volunteers.

[i] This park unit does not charge an entrance fee. The revenue shown here is from sales of lifetime senior passes and the interagency annual pass that occurred at the park.

[j] The National Mall and Memorial Parks has the following 12 national park units: Constitution Gardens, Ford's Theatre National Historic Site, Franklin D. Roosevelt Memorial, Korean War Veterans Memorial, Lincoln Memorial National Memorial, Martin Luther King, Jr. Memorial, National Mall, Pennsylvania Avenue National Historic Site, Thomas Jefferson Memorial, Vietnam Veterans Memorial, Washington Monument, and World War II Memorial.

[k] This park unit does not charge an entrance fee. The revenue shown here is from sales of lifetime senior passes and the interagency annual pass that occurred at the park.

# APPENDIX III: PARK PROFILES ON SELECTED NATIONAL PARK UNITS

The following figures provide a summary of selected information we collected during interviews with park officials and information we reviewed about individual parks' recreation fees, commercial service fees, and philanthropic partnerships.

- Recreation fees include entrance fees and amenity fees for certain equipment and services, such as campgrounds.
- Commercial service fees include franchise fees, commercial use authorizations, and rents.
- The Park Service is also authorized to develop agreements with nonprofit partner groups, known as friends groups and cooperating associations.

Source: National Park Service (photo). | GAO-16-166

## Antietam National Battlefield

### Background

Located in Sharpsburg, Maryland, this park preserves the battlefield where 23,000 soldiers were killed, wounded, or missing on September 17, 1862. The Battle of Antietam is considered the bloodiest 1-day battle in American history.

### Recreation fees

#### Entrance fees

**Does the park charge entrance fees?** Yes

The park sells annual passes and charges per vehicle and per person fees.

**How have these fees changed?**

In 2015, annual passes increased from $20 to $30, per vehicle fees increased from $6 to $10, and per person fees increased from $4 to $5.

#### Amenity fees

**Does the park charge amenity fees?** Yes

The park charges fees for camping.

### Commercial service fees

#### Concessions contracts

**Does the park have any concessions contracts?** No

Park officials told us they are hesitant to overly commercialize the park.

#### Leases

**Does the park have leases?** Yes

The park leases one historic house for residential uses. In addition, park officials are considering converting special use permits for farmland into leases.

### Philanthropic partnerships

#### Friends group

**Does the park have a friends group?** No

Park officials told us that at as of 2015 they do not plan on trying to establish a friends group due to staffing capacity at the park.

#### Cooperating association

**Does the park have a cooperating association?** Yes

Eastern National operates a bookstore in the visitor center and provides private tours for a fee.

Source: GAO summary of National Park Service information. | GAO-16-166

Figure 9. Antietam National Battlefield.

Source: National Park Service (photo). | GAO-16-166

## Cape Hatteras Group

### Background

The Cape Hatteras Group manages three parks in North Carolina: Cape Hatteras National Seashore; Fort Raleigh National Historic Site; and Wright Brothers National Memorial.

### Recreation fees

#### Entrance fees

**Does the group charge entrance fees?** Yes

Wright Brothers National Memorial sells an annual pass and charges a per person fee.

**How have these fees changed?**

In 2015, annual passes increased from $20 to $30 and per person fees increased from $4 to $7.

#### Amenity fees

**Does the group charge amenity fees?** Yes

The park charges campground, lighthouse climbing, interpretive, boat docking, and off-road vehicle permit fees.

### Commercial service fees

#### Concessions contracts

**Does the group have concessions contracts?** Yes

Cape Hatteras National Seashore has two contracts—one for a recreational pier and another for a fishing center. To increase revenues, park officials told us they are considering adding services and raising the franchise fee when the fishing center contract expires.

#### Leases

**Does the group have leases?** No

### Philanthropic partnerships

#### Friends group

**Does the group have a friends group?** Yes

In 2014, First Flight Society affiliated with Wright Brothers National Memorial and has provided in-kind donations.

#### Cooperating association

**Does the group have a cooperating association?** Yes

Eastern National operates bookstores in all three parks, and provides cash and in-kind donations.

Source: GAO summary of National Park Service information. | GAO-16-166

Figure 10. Cape Hatteras Group.

Sources: Nathan Kostegian; National Park Service (photo). | GAO-16-166

## Denali National Park and Preserve

### Background

Located in Alaska, this park spans 6 million acres of wildland, and features North America's tallest peak, Mount Denali. The park preserves low-elevation taiga forest, high alpine tundra, and snowy mountains.

### Recreation fees

#### Entrance fees

**Does the park charge entrance fees?** Yes

The park charges a per person fee.

**How have these fees changed?**

In 2012, the park's $20 per vehicle fee converted to a $10 per person fee.

#### Amenity fees

**Does the park charge amenity fees?** Yes

The park charges campground and mountain use fees.

### Commercial service fees

#### Concessions contracts

**Does the park have concessions contracts?** Yes

The park has 19 concessions contracts, including one contract for a dining facility, campground, bus service, and store. To increase revenues, park officials increased the franchise fee when this contract was competed in 2015.

#### Leases

**Does the park have leases?** No

Park officials told us they do not believe the park's unused facilities can be leased.

### Philanthropic partnerships

#### Friends groups

**Does the park have a friends group?** No

The park does not have an active friends group, but a small group is forming to support mountain rescue operations, as of September 2015.

#### Cooperating association

**Does the park have a cooperating association?** Yes

Alaska Geographic operates three retail outlets and offers fee-based programming at the park.

Source: GAO summary of National Park Service information. | GAO-16-166

Figure 11. Denali National Park and Preserve.

Sources: Nathan Kostegian; National Park Service (photo). | GAO-16-166

## Eugene O'Neill National Historic Site

### Background

Located in Danville, California, this park preserves the site where Pulitzer Prize-winning American playwright Eugene O'Neill authored some of his most memorable plays: *The Iceman Cometh*, *A Moon for the Misbegotten*, and *Long Day's Journey Into Night*.

### Recreation fees

#### Entrance fees

**Does the park charge entrance fees?** No

Park officials told us this is due to the park's location on a private road managed by a homeowners association.

#### Amenity fees

**Does the park charge amenity fees?** No

Park officials told us that they are hesitant to charge amenity fees because doing so could negatively impact visitation.

### Commercial service fees

#### Concessions contracts

**Does the park have concessions contracts?** No

Park officials told us that none of the park's programs warrant food or other concessions.

#### Leases

**Does the park have leases?** No

Park officials told us that the park has no facilities to lease.

### Philanthropic partnerships

#### Friends groups

**Does the park have a friends group?** Yes

The Eugene O'Neill Foundation provides interpretive support by organizing theater festivals and programs. The group sells tickets to some of these events, the proceeds from which support park activities and improvements.

#### Cooperating association

**Does the park have a cooperating association?** Yes

Western National Park Association operates a bookstore at the park.

Source: GAO summary of National Park Service information. | GAO-16-166

Figure 12. Eugene O'Neill National Historic Site.

Sources: Nathan Kostegian; National Park Service (photo). | GAO-16-166

## Fort McHenry National Monument and Historic Shrine

### Background

Located in Baltimore, Maryland, this park preserves the site where the Battle of Baltimore was waged in 1814, inspiring Francis Scott Key to write the national anthem, "The Star-Spangled Banner."

### Recreation fees

#### Entrance fees

■ **Does the park charge entrance fees?** Yes

The park sells an annual pass and charges a per person fee.

■ **How have these fees changed?**

In 2015, the annual pass increased from $30 to $40, and the per person fee increased from $7 to $10.

#### Amenity fees

■ **Does the park charge amenity fees?** No

Park officials told us that there are not any specialized equipment services or services provided at the park not included as part of the entrance fee.

### Commercial service fees

#### Concessions contracts

■ **Does the park have concessions contracts?** Yes

There is one concessions contract for a bookstore.

#### Leases

■ **Does the park have leases?** No

This is because the park lacks staff to manage a leasing program, according to park officials.

### Philanthropic partnerships

#### Friends groups

■ **Does the park have a friends group?** Yes

Living Classrooms Foundation provides in-kind donations, such as transportation for school children, that support educational activities.

#### Cooperating association

■ **Does the park have a cooperating association?** Yes

Living Classrooms Foundation sells books.

Source: GAO summary of National Park Service information. | GAO-16-166

Figure 13. Fort McHenry National Monument and Historic Shrine.

Sources: Brian Hall, National Park Service (photo). | GAO-16-166

# National Mall and Memorial Parks

## Background

Located in Located in Washington, D.C., the National Mall and Memorial Parks has 12 national park units, including the National Mall, Vietnam Veterans Memorial, and Washington Monument.

## Recreation fees

### Entrance fees

**Does the park charge entrance fees?** No

Park units are not allowed to charge entrance fees by law.[a]

### Amenity fees

**Does the park charge amenity fees?** Yes

The park charges for permits to use picnic areas and volleyball courts. In the fall of 2015, parking fees will be charged along the Mall.

## Commercial service fees

### Concessions contracts

**Does the park have concessions contracts?** Yes

The park has four concessions contracts for a food and beverage operation, golf course, bus tour, and food carts. Park officials told us the franchise fee for the bus tour increased from 3 to 8 percent when the new contract was signed in 2015.

### Leases

**Does the park have leases?** No

## Philanthropic partnerships

### Friends groups

**Does the park have a friends group?** Yes

The Trust for the National Mall is the primary friends group. However, the park has over 150 agreements with other partners to help maintain memorials and green spaces throughout Washington, D.C.

### Cooperating association

**Does the park have a cooperating association?** Yes

Eastern National operates bookstores at five locations, including the Jefferson and Lincoln Memorials.

Source: GAO summary of National Park Service information. | GAO-16-166

[a] 16 U.S.C. § 459c-5(e) (2015).

Figure 20. National Mall and Memorial Parks.

Source: National Park Service (photo). | GAO-16-166

## Point Reyes National Seashore

### Background

Located in Point Reyes Station, California, this park spans 70,000 acres and covers expansive sand beaches, open grasslands, brushy hillsides, and forested ridges with over 1,500 species of plants and animals.

### Recreation fees

#### Entrance fees

**Does the park charge entrance fees?** No

The park is prohibited by law from charging entrance fees.[a]

#### Amenity fees

**Does the park charge amenity fees?** Yes

The park charges for backcountry camping and a shuttle bus.

### Commercial service fees

#### Concessions contracts

**Does the park have concessions contracts?** Yes

The park has four contracts for horse stables, a horse camp, a hostel, and an operation that sells limited convenience items. Park officials said they are hesitant to raise franchise fee rates, since the park's concessioners provide critical services to visitors, but do not earn a lot of revenue.

#### Leases

**Does the park have leases?** No

Park officials told us the park does not have any buildings that are in adequate shape to lease.

### Philanthropic partnerships

#### Friends groups

**Does the park have a friends group?** No

However, the park's cooperating association—Point Reyes National Seashore Association—has raised funds and provided in-kind donations to the park.

#### Cooperating association

**Does the park have a cooperating association?** Yes

Point Reyes National Seashore Association operates bookstores and provides educational programming.

Source: GAO summary of National Park Service information. | GAO-16-166

[a] 16 U.S.C. § 459c-5(e) (2015).

Figure 21. Point Reyes National Seashore.

Source: National Park Service (photo). | GAO-16-166

## Port Chicago Naval Magazine National Memorial

### Background

Located on an active military base in California's Suisun Bay, this park commemorates the site where 320 men died when two ships being loaded with munitions exploded in 1944. Their deaths called attention to safety problems and naval segregation policies.

### Recreation fees

#### Entrance fees

**Does the park charge entrance fees?** No

The park does not manage any fee collection sites at this park, which is located on an active U.S. military base.

#### Amenity fees

**Does the park charge amenity fees?** No

The park does not issue permits at this site.

### Commercial service fees

#### Concessions contracts

**Does the park have concessions contracts?** No

Park officials said they are not likely to develop such contracts because Park Service does not manage facilities at this site.

#### Leases

**Does the park have leases?** No

Park officials told us that leasing is not an option because Park Service does not manage any facilities at this site.

### Philanthropic partnerships

#### Friends groups

**Does the park have a friends group?** Yes

Friends of Port Chicago Memorial, which helped create the park, raises funds to support the park's annual memorial event.

#### Cooperating association

**Does the park have a cooperating association?** No

There is no visitor center or facility at which to operate a bookstore.

Source: GAO summary of National Park Service information. | GAO-16-166

Figure 22. Port Chicago Naval Magazine National Memorial.

Source: National Park Service (photo). | GAO-16-166

## Rosie the Riveter/WWII Home Front National Historic Park

### Background

Located in Richmond, California, this park commemorates the industrial boom that occurred on the home front during World War II, impacting women and minorities in the workforce. The park is composed of 16 affiliated sites, none of which are owned by the federal government.

### Recreation fees

Entrance fees

- **Does the park charge entrance fees?** No

Park officials told us that they do not charge fees because the federal government does not own property at the park.

Amenity fees

- **Does the park charge amenity fees?** No

Park officials told us that they cannot charge amenity fees because the federal government does not own or manage property at this park.

### Commercial service fees

Concessions contracts

- **Does the park have concessions contracts?** No

Park officials told us that they cannot develop concessions contracts because the federal government does not own or manage property at this park.

Leases

- **Does the park have leases?** No

Park officials told us that they do not lease buildings because the federal government does not own property at the park.

### Philanthropic partnerships

Friends groups

- **Does the park have a friends group?** Yes

Rosie the Riveter Trust has raised funds and provided in-kind donations, such as a collection of artifacts for display.

Cooperating association

- **Does the park have a cooperating association?** Yes

Rosie the Riveter Trust operates a bookstore, provides volunteers, and provides interpretive services.

Source: GAO summary of National Park Service information. | GAO-16-166

Figure 23. Rosie the Riveter/WWII Home Front National Historic Park.

Source: National Park Service (photo). | GAO-16-166

## San Francisco Maritime National Historical Park

### Background

Located near San Francisco's Fisherman's Wharf neighborhood, this park offers Pacific Coast maritime history, historic buildings and grounds, and urban recreation.

### Recreation fees

#### Entrance fees

**Does the park charge entrance fees?** Yes

The park sells an annual pass and charges a per person fee.

**How have these fees changed?**

In 2015, the annual pass increased from $20 to $40, and the per person fee increased from $5 to $10.

#### Amenity fees

**Does the park charge amenity fees?** No

As of October 2015, the park does not charge amenity fees, but officials said they are considering charging fees to boats that dock at the park.

### Commercial service fees

#### Concessions contracts

**Does the park have concessions contracts?** No

#### Leases

**Does the park have leases?** Yes

The park has two leases—one with a hotel and another for a dry dock. Park officials said they are considering raising the rent for the dry dock when the lease expires.

### Philanthropic partnerships

#### Friends groups

**Does the park have a friends group?** Yes

Friends of the San Francisco Maritime Museum Library supports the park's archives.

#### Cooperating association

**Does the park have a cooperating association?** Yes

San Francisco Maritime National Historical Park Association offers interpretive and educational programs, such as shipbuilding classes. Western National Parks Association also runs a store at the park.

Source: GAO summary of National Park Service information. | GAO-16-166

Figure 24. San Francisco Maritime National Historical Park.

Sources: Neal Lewis; National Park Service (photo) | GAO-16-166

## Shenandoah National Park

### Background

Located in Virginia, this park preserves 200,000 acres of land featuring eastern deciduous forest, abundant wildlife, streams, waterfalls and over 80,000 acres of congressionally designated wilderness.

### Recreation fees

#### Entrance fees

**Does the park charge entrance fees?** Yes

The park charges all four types: annual, vehicle, person, motorcycle.

**How have these fees changed?**

In 2015, annual passes increased from $30 to $40, per vehicle fees increased from $15 to $20, per person fees increased from $8 to $10, and per motorcycle fees increased from $10 to $15. In addition, starting in 2017, Park Service has approved the park to increase annual passes to $50, per vehicle fees to $25, and per motorcycle fees to $20.

#### Amenity fees

**Does the park charge amenity fees?** Yes

It charges interpretive fees for ranger-guided tours of Rapidan Camp, President Hoover's former retreat.

### Commercial service fees

#### Concessions contracts

**Does the park have concessions contracts?** Yes

The park has one contract for lodging, horseback riding, food and beverage, convenience store, shower, and laundry services. Park officials told us they would like to increase franchise fees the next time the agency competes this contract in 2022.

#### Leases

**Does the park have leases?** No

Park officials told us that they have evaluated the park's leasing options but said they do not believe that their facilities have leasing potential, since all of their buildings are utilized.

### Philanthropic partnerships

#### Friends groups

**Does the park have a friends group?** Yes

Shenandoah Trust raises funds for the park.

#### Cooperating association

**Does the park have a cooperating association?** Yes

Shenandoah National Park Association operates three sales outlets in the park.

Source: GAO summary of National Park Service information. | GAO-16-166

Figure 25. Shenandoah National Park.

Sources: Jeffrey Trust; National Park Service (photo). | GAO-16-166

## Yosemite National Park

### Background

Located in the Sierra Mountains of California, this park is best known for its sheer granite walls and waterfalls. Within its nearly 1,200 square miles, there are deep valleys, grand meadows, giant sequoias, and vast wilderness areas.

### Recreation fees

#### Entrance fees

■ **Does the park charge entrance fees?** Yes

The park charges all four types: annual, vehicle, person, motorcycle.

■ **How have these fees changed?**

By 2017, the annual pass will increase from $40 to $60, the per vehicle pass will increase from $20 to $30, the per person pass will increase from $10 to $15, and the per motorcycle pass will increase from $10 to $25.

#### Amenity fees

■ **Does the park charge amenity fees?** Yes

The park charges for camping.

### Commercial service fees

#### Concessions contracts

■ **Does the park have concessions contracts?** Yes

The park has three concessions contracts for: a lodging and food and beverage operation; an art gallery; and a market.

#### Leases

■ **Does the park have leases?** No

However, park officials said they may consider converting one concessions contract into a lease when that contract expires.

### Philanthropic partnerships

#### Friends groups

■ **Does the park have a friends group?** Yes

Yosemite Conservancy provided over $11 million in cash and in-kind support to the park in 2014, according to park officials.

#### Cooperating association

■ **Does the park have a cooperating association?** Yes

Yosemite Conservancy operates eight retail outlets, coordinates volunteers, and provides interpretive support through publishing, arts, and theater programming. Another organization, called Nature Bridge, provides environmental programs to students.

Source: GAO summary of National Park Service information. | GAO-16-166

Figure 26. Yosemite National Park.

## End Notes

[1] GAO, *National Park Service: Major Operations Funding Trends and How Selected Park Units Responded to Those Trends for Fiscal Years 2001 Through 2005,* GAO-06-431 (Washington, D.C.: Mar. 31, 2006).

[2] National Park Service, *Fiscal Year 2014 Deferred Maintenance Reports* (Mar. 23, 2015).

[3] In its budget justification, the Park Service calls these funding streams discretionary and mandatory appropriations. It uses "discretionary appropriations" to refer to funding that comes from the annual appropriations process while it uses "mandatory appropriations" to refer to funding that includes fees and donations.

[4] We selected this period because it was the most recent 10-year period for which data were available, and 10 years of data would allow us to identify any trends. OMB's MAX Information System is a database used to support OMB's federal management and budget processes. The system collects, validates, analyzes, models, and publishes information relating to government-wide management and budgeting activities.

[5] We adjusted nominal dollars using the fiscal year chain-weighted gross domestic price index, with 2014 as the base year.

[6] GAO, *Federal User Fees: A Design Guide*, GAO-08-386SP (Washington, D.C.: May 29, 2008). To develop this user guide, we reviewed economic and policy literature on federal and nonfederal user fees, including our prior work on user fees.

[7] GAO, *Standards for Internal Control in the Federal Government*, GAO/AIMD-00-21.3.1 (Washington, D.C.: Nov. 1999).

[8] Act of August 25, 1916, ch. 408, § 1, 39 Stat. 535, 535 (codified as amended at 54 U.S.C. §§ 100101, 100301). The 1916 legislation is commonly referred to as the National Park Service Organic Act.

[9] The Park Service has also occasionally received funding in other accounts. For example, the agency received funding in a Centennial Challenge account in 2008 and 2015 and in a Park Partnership Project Grant account in 2010.

[10] Until September 30, 2015, the Land and Water Conservation Fund accumulated revenue from the federal motorboat fuel tax and surplus property sales. To supplement these sources, the fund accumulated revenue from oil and gas leases on the Outer Continental Shelf.

[11] Pub. L. No. 108-447, div. J. tit. VIII, 118 Stat. 3377 (2004) (codified as amended at 16 U.S.C. §§ 6801-6814 (2015)).

[12] Pub. L. No. 105-391, tit. IV, 112 Stat. 3503 (codified as amended at 54 U.S.C. §§ 101911 – 101926 (2015)).

[13] 54 U.S.C. § 102102 (2015).

[14] 54 U.S.C. §§ 100725, 101101 (2015).

[15] 54 U.S.C. § 101702 (2015).

[16] Broadly speaking, interpretive services involve providing educational information to visitors about the park units. Examples of these services include providing information to visitors about animals or plants in a park unit.

[17] Pub. L. No. 91-537, 84 Stat. 472, codified as amended at 54 U.S.C. § 102301 (2015).

[18] These funding sources are outside the scope of this review.

[19] American Recovery and Reinvestment Act of 2009, Pub. L. No. 111-5, 123 Stat. 115.

[20] The remaining 28 percent of funding in this category include funding from the Department of the Treasury for certain pension payments for the U.S. Park Police ($45.5 million in fiscal year 2014), rents that the Park Service collects for employee housing ($23.1 million in fiscal year 2014), and fees collected to operate public transportation systems in parks units ($17.4 million in fiscal year 2014).

[21] Department of the Interior and Department of Agriculture, *Implementation of the Federal Lands Recreation Act: Triennial Report to Congress* (May 2012).

[22] Special recreation permit fees are also collected under FLREA by the Park Service, but these accounted on average for about 0.22 percent of total recreation fees during the period we examined.

[23] National Park Service, *Reference Manual 22A: Recreation Fee Collection* (February 2014).

[24] According to Park Service officials, during this time period, some concessioners also deposited funds into Concessions Improvement Accounts in accordance with contracts entered into under the National Park Service Concessions Policy Act (Pub. L. No. 89-249, 79 Stat. 969 (1965)), which was repealed by the National Park Service Concessions Management Improvement Act of 1998. According to the Park Service's budget justification, these funds are available only for expenditure by the concessioner, with park unit approval, for required capital improvements that directly support the facilities used and services provided by the concessioner. These funds are excluded from our review because they are not available for the Park Service's use.

[25] In this report, we exclude rents collected from Park Service employees for housing from our analysis.

[26] For commercial use authorizations, more parks may have started reporting their commercial use revenues during this period. According to Park Service officials, the Park Service began collecting park-level data on commercial use authorizations on a voluntary basis in 2009.

[27] The Park Service calculates the cash value of their volunteers' work by multiplying the number of hours the volunteers work by the Independent Sector's estimate of the value of volunteer time, which was $23.07/hour for 2014. The Independent Sector is a leadership network for the nonprofit and philanthropic community.

[28] Hurricane Sandy closed several park units in the northeast for certain periods of time. The 2013 federal government shutdown closed all national park units for a period of 16 days.

[29] The 2006 fee schedule stemmed from a 2001 study by McKinsey and Company that said that the Park Service should standardize its entrance fees.

[30] Not all park units that charge entrance fees charge all four types of entrance fees. For example, certain parks may not charge vehicle or motorcycle fees because they do not have roads.

[31] GAO/AIMD-00-21.3.1.

[32] National Park Service, *Reference Manual 22A: Recreation Fee Collection*, section 3.2.4.

[33] GAO-08-386SP.

[34] National Park Service, *Management Policies*, (2006).

[35] Office of Inspector General, U.S. Department of the Interior, *Review of National Park Service's Recreation Fee Program*, C-IN-NPS-0012-2013 (February 2015).

[36] FLREA is currently set to expire September 30, 2016. 16 U.S.C. § 6809 (2015).

[37] There is a long history of collecting entrance fees starting in 1908, when Mount Rainier National Park began collecting entrance fees. In 1939, fee collection became the general policy of the executive branch. The Land and Water Conservation Fund Act of 1965 specifically authorized certain federal agencies, including the Park Service, to collect entrance and use fees, and, within certain parameters, to sell an annual interagency vehicle entrance pass (Pub. L. No. 88-578 § 2, 78 Stat. 897, 897-899). In 1996, Congress authorized the Recreational Fee Demonstration Program through the Omnibus Consolidated Rescissions and Appropriations Act of 1996, requiring the Secretary of the Interior to implement a pilot fee program at four land management agencies: the Park Service, the Bureau of Land Management, the U.S. Fish and Wildlife Service, and the U.S. Department of Agriculture Forest Service (Pub. L. No. 104-134, § 315, 110 Stat. 1321, 1321-200-1321-202).

[38] 16 U.S.C. § 410hh-2 (2015). FLREA excepts Denali National Park and Preserve from this prohibition. 16 U.S.C. § 6802(d)(3)(G) (2015).

[39] 16 U.S.C. § 6802(d)(3)(C) (2015).

[40] 16 U.S.C. § 459c-5(e) (2015).

[41] Entrance fees had just been charged at the Great Falls area in the park and, in January 2015, the park proposed charging entrance fees at all areas of the park outside the District of Columbia.

[42] Of these agencies, the Park Service collects the majority of recreation fees. In fiscal year 2011, the Park Service collected about two-thirds of the total recreation fees collected ($172.4 million of the $260.6 million). See *Implementation of the Federal Lands Recreation Act: Triennial Report to Congress.*

[43] Office of Inspector General, U.S. Department of the Interior, *Review of National Park Service's Recreation Fee Program.*

[44] National Park Service Centennial Act, H.R. 3556, 114th Cong. § 602 (2015).

[45] The amount of additional revenue could be lower if the amount of the price increase deters seniors from purchasing the pass.

[46] GAO-08-386SP.

[47] The Concessions Act states that a concessions contract shall provide for payment to the government a franchise fee or other monetary consideration, upon consideration of the probable value to the concessioner of the privileges granted by the contract, and that "probable value" should be based on a reasonable opportunity for net profit in relation to capital invested and the obligations of the contract.

[48] We conducted this analysis using data on 25 contracts that were managed by Park Service headquarters and awarded between fiscal years 2005 and 2014. These contracts are a subset of the Park Service's total concessions contracts and generally represent the Park Service's largest concessions contracts.

[49] The value of LSI is the initial value of the capital improvement adjusted for inflation minus depreciation. When new contracts incur more than $10,000,000 in LSI, the value of LSI can be calculated using straight-line depreciation or by an alternative formula consistent with the law's objectives.

[50] In payment in lieu of rent arrangements, the Park Service agrees to waive or charge a reduced rent in exchange for the lessee providing agreed upon services, maintenance projects, such as roof repairs, or capital improvements, such as building renovations.

[51] Among other things, an existing parking lot will be removed, and the area's natural wetlands will be restored as part of the project.

[52] Of this $15 million, $10 million was to be transferred from prior year unobligated balances.

[53] Geographic features are named by the U.S. Board on Geographic Names. Therefore, naming such features is outside the Park Service's domain and is therefore unaffected by this waiver.

[54] The IRS Form 990 is an annual information return required to be filed with the IRS by most tax-exempt organizations. It provides information on the filing organization's mission, programs, and finances. The Park Service gathers information from the Form 990s from a website called Guidestar, which collects information on nonprofit organizations.

[55] The Park Service only has cash and in-kind contributions data available from friends groups that file IRS Form 990s. Smaller friends groups—ones that receive less than $50,000 in gross receipts in a given tax year—are not required to file these forms, and, therefore, the Park Service does not have an estimate of their contributions.

[56] OMB's MAX Information System is a database used to support OMB's federal management and budget processes. The system collects, validates, analyzes, models, and publishes information relating to OMB's government-wide management and budgeting activities.

[57] We adjusted nominal dollars using the fiscal year chain-weighted gross domestic price index, with 2014 as the base year.

[58] Pub. L. No. 108-447, div. J. tit. VIII, 118 Stat. 3377 (2004) (codified as amended at 16 U.S.C. §§ 6801-6814 (2015)).

[59] Pub. L. No. 105-391, tit. IV, 112 Stat. 3503 (codified as amended at 54 U.S.C. §§ 101911 – 101926 (2015)).

[60] Pub. L. No. 91-537, 84 Stat. 472 (codified as amended at 54 U.S.C. § 102301 (2015).

[61] See GAO-08-386SP. To develop this user guide, we reviewed economic and policy literature on federal and nonfederal user fees, including our prior work on user fees.

[62] GAO, *Standards for Internal Control in the Federal Government*, GAO/AIMD-00-21.3.1 (Washington, D.C.: Nov. 1999).

[63] In some cases, some of these park units were managed together by the same administrative team. For example, the National Mall and Memorial Parks manages twelve park units and the Cape Hatteras Group manages three park units. For the purposes of the tally of parks units we contacted, we counted these as a total of 15 park units, since we discussed the revenue streams in place at all of these park units.

In: National Park Service
Editor: Claire Cohen
ISBN: 978-1-63485-819-9


*Chapter 3*

# REVIEW OF NATIONAL PARK SERVICE'S RECREATION FEE PROGRAM*

***Office of Inspector General***

Memorandum FEB 1 9 2015

From: Mary L. Kendall

Subject: Final Audit Report – Review of National Park Service's Recreation Fee Program

Report No. C-IN-NPS-0012-2013

This report, part of a larger portfolio of our work to identify opportunities where the U.S. Department of the Interior can maximize income from its revenue-generating programs, presents the results of our audit of the National Park Service's (NPS) Recreation Fee Program. NPS' recreation fees can go toward a vast array of projects that improve the visitor experience, from facility maintenance and repair to visitor services and education. Our objective was to highlight areas in which NPS can increase its recreation fee revenue, and we focused on the agency's three

* This is an edited, reformatted and augmented version of Report No. C-IN-NPS-0012-2013, issued by the U.S. Department of the Interior, February 2015.

biggest revenue-generating mechanisms: entrance fees, interagency park passes, and commercial bus tour fees.

We found several areas in which NPS is missing opportunities to maximize its fee revenue:

1. Although NPS implemented an entrance fee model in 2006, it had been working under a self-imposed fee moratorium from 2008 through most of 2014—just short of one-fifth of entrance-fee-charging park units charged according to the NPS model.
2. While park units can ask to update their fees, NPS' lengthy process likely deterred them from making the attempt.
3. NPS issued almost a million interagency park passes in 2012 alone, and well over two-thirds of the passes were free or substantially discounted.
4. NPS has not updated its fee schedule for commercial tour buses in 16 years, and parks that charge tour operators per a commercial use authorization have only interim guidance from which to manage the arrangements.

In this final report, we offer six recommendations encouraging NPS to assess its current fee policies, prices, and models to determine where it can make updates. We learned shortly before issuing our draft report, however, that NPS had already begun addressing some of the issues we identified. After reviewing the draft report, NPS concurred with our recommendations and provided more information on the status of each.

Based on the information NPS provided, we consider recommendations 1 and 3 to be implemented, recommendations 2 and 4 to be unresolved, and recommendations 5 and 6 to be resolved but not implemented. We are referring recommendations 2, 4, 5, and 6 to the Assistant Secretary for Policy, Management and Budget to track their implementation.

The legislation creating the Office of Inspector General requires that we report to Congress semiannually on all audit, inspection, and evaluation reports issued; actions taken to implement our recommendations; and recommendations that have not been implemented. If you have any questions regarding this report, please contact me at 202-208-5745.

# RESULTS IN BRIEF

We examined potential opportunities for the National Park Service (NPS) to increase its recreation program revenues—a subject of particular relevance at a time when Federal agencies have faced mounting fiscal pressures. We focused on NPS' three largest recreation-revenue-generating mechanisms: park-unit entrance fees, interagency passes, and commercial bus tour fees. Park units (e.g., national parks, national recreation areas, or national monuments) use the revenues from these mechanisms for projects that enhance the visitor experience, such as facility maintenance and visitor information and services.

We found the following:

- NPS froze entrance fees shortly after implementing a new fee model in 2006. Today only 24 out of 131 entrance-fee-charging park units charge fees according to the model. NPS could collect approximately $28 million more in fees each year just by fully implementing the current fee model.
- Park units can change their fees if a "compelling" reason exists, but our review of NPS memoranda showed that the NPS Director had not defined alignment with the fee model as a compelling reason to raise fees. Furthermore, NPS' process for changing recreation fees can take well over a year, and the time and effort needed to go through the process had likely deterred park units from attempting to update their fees.
- Free and substantially discounted entrance passes represent missed opportunities for revenue. NPS issues three types of free annual passes— one for active military personnel, one for individuals who have volunteered 250 or more hours on Federal recreation lands, and one for individuals with permanent disabilities—plus a $10 lifetime pass for citizens 62 years of age and older. Over 695,000 of these passes are issued each year.
- NPS implemented its current fee schedule for commercial bus tours in 1998 and has not updated it since. NPS could see another $4 million to $5 million annually if it increased the commercial bus tour fee rate by roughly 30 percent.
- Park units sometimes charge commercial bus tour operators a commercial use authorization (CUA) fee rather than following the fee

schedule. Issuing CUAs is a cost-recovery activity, but for almost a decade NPS has had only interim guidance in place for managing CUAs. This could be reducing opportunities for NPS to recover costs.

NPS' authority to charge fees under the Federal Lands Recreation Enhancement Act will end in 2016, and this legislative uncertainty hampers NPS' flexibility in managing its Recreation Fee Program. We offer six recommendations encouraging NPS to assess its current fee policies, prices, and models and to determine where it can consider making updates. Shortly before we issued this report, we were pleased to learn that NPS has already begun addressing some of our recommendations.

# INTRODUCTION

## Objective

This audit is part of a larger portfolio of Office of Inspector General work focusing on maximizing revenue opportunities in U.S. Department of the Interior (DOI) revenue-generating programs and operations. Our audit objective was to highlight opportunities where the National Park Service (NPS) can increase recreation program revenues. We focused on NPS' three largest revenue-generating mechanisms: entrance fees, interagency passes, and commercial bus tour fees. For the audit's scope and methodology, see Appendix 1.

## Background

Enacted in December 2004, the Federal Lands Recreation Enhancement Act (FLREA) granted five Federal agencies—the Bureau of Land Management, the Bureau of Reclamation, the U.S. Fish and Wildlife Service, NPS, and the U.S. Forest Service–the authority to establish, modify, charge, and collect recreation fees at Federal recreational lands and waters. Recreation fees include entrance fees, standard amenity fees, expanded amenity fees, and special recreation permits. According to the 2012 "Triennial Report to Congress," NPS accounted for over 65 percent of all agency FLREA revenue.

Under FLREA, a park unit (such as a national park, a national recreation area, or a national monument) may keep 80 percent of the recreation fee revenue it collects. The remaining 20 percent goes into a centralized account and is allocated across all park units based on project proposals and NPS priorities. Fee revenue can only be used for projects that are directly related to visitors and the visitor experience, including—

- repair, maintenance, and facility enhancement;
- interpretation, visitor information, visitor services, visitor needs assessments, and signs;
- habitat restoration directly related to wildlife-dependent recreation that is limited to hunting, fishing, wildlife observation, or photography;
- law enforcement related to public use and recreation; and
- direct operating or capital costs associated with the Recreation Fee Program.

Much of NPS' recreation fee revenue comes from entrance fees, with $82.5 million collected in fiscal year (FY) 2012. NPS manages 401 park unit sites and collects entrance fees at a little less than a third of them (131). The Intermountain and Pacific West regions, on which we focused our work and site visits, account for more than half (72) of all entrance-fee-charging park units and contain all 10 of NPS' top-fee-level parks.

Visitors are charged an entrance fee when they enter a park unit. The fee can be an annual park pass, a per-vehicle fee, a per-person fee, or a motorcycle fee. NPS' current entrance fee model is rooted in a study it commissioned in 2001 to develop options for enhancing recreation revenue programs. The study found that NPS fees varied, even among similar parks, and that parks perceived a need for greater simplicity and consistency. The group that conducted the analysis provided a variety of options for improvements to NPS' program, mainly simplifying the fee pricing structure by grouping similar parks around one price point. In response, NPS spent the next 5 years developing the four-tiered entrance fee model in place today.

NPS also distributes or sells a variety of interagency passes established under FLREA that provide holders with free or extremely discounted access to Federal recreation areas. NPS manages the interagency pass program for all five FLREA agencies. The $10 Senior Pass and the free Access Pass for individuals with permanent disabilities are both specifically designated in the law. To assist Federal agencies in pricing the Annual Pass, NPS commissioned a study in 2006, the results of which serve as the basis for the current $80 fee.

Interagency pass sales (from Senior Passes and Annual Passes) brought in some $26 million in FY 2012.

Commercial bus tour fees generated the third highest recreation-related revenue in FY 2012, with a total of $15.4 million. The Land and Water Conservation Fund Act of 1965 (LWCFA) was amended in 1993 by adding the stipulation that commercial tour vehicles would be charged a fee upon entering any entrance-feecharging park unit.[1] The amendment also notes that these fees may be reasonably adjusted on a periodic basis. NPS assembled a task force that worked with the commercial bus tour industry to develop and implement a fee structure. After two relatively unsuccessful implementation efforts and subsequent revisions, NPS finally adopted a flat-rate commercial bus tour fee schedule in 1998. This schedule remains in use today.

FLREA is authorized until September 2016, having received an extension from its original sunset date of December 2014. Draft language updating many sections of FLREA has been discussed before Congress but not yet adopted. In addition, NPS could see an increase to its operational budgets in FY 2015 from its budget proposal to prepare parks and public lands in advance of NPS' 100th anniversary in 2016. Given this legislative uncertainty and potential influx of operational funds, NPS' approach to introducing or changing fees has been, understandably, cautious. Still, NPS faces considerable, persistent fiscal challenges, and it needs reliable funding to address maintenance backlogs and projects that directly affect the park visitor experience.

# FINDINGS

## A Self-Imposed Moratorium Has Limited NPS' Ability to Add or Increase Entrance Fees

When NPS implemented its entrance fee model in 2006, the model standardized entrance fees across four different park groupings based on the park units' designations (Figures 1 and 2).

In 2008, however, shortly after parks began to implement the new fee model, the NPS Director imposed a moratorium that froze entrance fees at 2007 levels. The current NPS Director maintained the freeze from 2008 until late in 2014.

| Group | Description |
|---|---|
| 1 | National historic sites, national military parks, national battlefields, national battlefield parks, national memorials or shrines, national preserves, parkways |
| 2 | National seashores, national recreation areas, national monuments, national lakeshores, national historical parks |
| 3 | National parks |
| 4 | National parks* |

*There are only 10 Group 4 parks: Bryce Canyon, Glacier, Grand Canyon, Grand Teton, Olympic, Rocky Mountain, Sequoia-Kings Canyon, Yellowstone, Yosemite, and Zion.

Figure 1. Park group descriptions. Source: NPS Reference Manual 22A: "Recreation Fee Collection" (April 2011).

| Group | Annual Pass | Per Vehicle | Per Person | Motorcycle |
|---|---|---|---|---|
| 1 | $20 | $10 | $5 | $5 |
| 2 | $30 | $15 | $7 | $10 |
| 3 | $40 | $20 | $10 | $15 |
| 4 | $50 | $25 | $12 | $20 |

Figure 2. Park group entrance fees. Source: NPS Reference Manual 22A: "Recreation Fee Collection" (April 2011).

Early on, the primary reason given for the freeze was concern over raising fees at a time when NPS had received an increase to its operational budgets to prepare for its upcoming centennial. Uncertainty also existed over the repeal or reauthorization of FLREA. In a 2012 memo related to 2013 fee changes, a justification for continuing the moratorium was absent altogether, illustrating a sentiment that park unit staff shared with us: NPS' cultural message seemed to be not to increase entrance fees.

Due to the short time between the fee model implementation and the moratorium, only 24 out of 131 park units have put in place entrance fees commensurate with the fee model. Every park unit we visited charged one or more of its entrance fees below the assigned level (Appendix 2). Motorcycle fees in particular vary widely by park unit, with some units charging per the fee model, others charging per-person rates, and still others charging per-vehicle rates.

NPS Recreation Fee Program staff estimates that NPS' annual revenue from entrance fees would increase by roughly $28 million if all fee-charging park units could fully implement the fee model (Appendix 3). We believe that

NPS might realize even more revenue if it also updated this model to account for inflation.

Another alternative would be to reconsider the current fee groupings for park units. For example, national recreation areas, such as Lake Mead or Glen Canyon, are categorized as Group 2 park units under the NPS fee model. As such, their entrance fees according to the current fee model are roughly 60 percent lower than fees for top-tier (Group 4) national parks such as Yellowstone, the Grand Canyon, or Yosemite. This is true even for national recreation areas that are similar in size, that have similar visitation levels (or vastly more, in the case of Lake Mead), and that host recreational uses that are often broader than those generally offered at parks (Appendix 4).[2] We spoke to more than one park employee who indicated that the current fee groupings were not realistic and that they should also account for other variables, such as the type of recreation taking place at the site or the type of visitors attracted (e.g., long-distance travelers vs. local residents).

**Recommendations**

We recommend that NPS:

1. Assess the need for continuing the freeze on fee increases and consider lifting the moratorium to allow park units to begin submitting requests to adjust fees to align with the current fee model; and
2. Begin the process of reevaluating the current fee model to determine necessary updates and establish intervals for periodic reviews to ensure the fee model remains up to date.

## NPS' Process for Changing Fees Is Onerous and Likely Deters Park Units from Updating Fees

Despite the fee moratorium, park units may request an exception to change their entrance fees if a "compelling" reason exists. FLREA requires agencies to involve the public when instituting or changing a recreation fee (including entrance fees); when introducing an entirely new fee at a site, the law mandates a 6-month public notification. NPS' own process for changing an entrance fee includes layers of internal review (from the park unit to the directorate) in addition to extensive public outreach. It can take well over a year from the time a park unit asks to engage in public outreach to the time it implements the new fee. It can take a few years to change an entrance fee to align with the current fee model, as a park may suggest phasing in a fee change to avoid an "extreme" increase.

Aligning entrance fees with the fee model is not considered a compelling reason to change an entrance fee, and the time and resources necessary to complete the fee-change process likely deters some parks from seeking fee increases. For example, in 2007, three national parks—Arches, Canyonlands, and Pinnacles— and Muir Woods National Monument completed, to positive effect, the time-consuming process of public outreach to increase fees in 2008. When NPS put the fee moratorium in place, however, Arches and Canyonlands were unable to implement their proposed fee increases, while Muir Woods only implemented part of what was to be a phased increase. The request from Pinnacles was forestalled by the regional director even before the moratorium was formally in place. Once a proposed fee increase is denied, the fee-change process would entail further public outreach before a new request could even go to the regional director for consideration, despite the work already accomplished. Today, each of these park units still charges entrance fees below the current fee model rates, and staff at each site expressed hesitancy at attempting the process again.

In 2009, Lake Mead requested an exception to the fee moratorium to begin the process of increasing its entrance fees to Group 2 levels, noting that its fees were not sufficient to operate its fee program. Fee staff at the park conducted a noteworthy amount of public outreach for a two-phased increase, with the first phase to take effect in 2011 and the second in 2014. Lake Mead received approval to implement the 2011 increase, but when it came time to implement the second phase, staff were told that they would have to start the fee-change process over. Staff told us that they simply did not have the time or resources to go through the process again.

**Recommendations**

We recommend that NPS:

3. Examine the fee-change process to determine where it can be streamlined and change it accordingly.

# FREE AND SUBSTANTIALLY DISCOUNTED INTERAGENCY PASSES REPRESENT MISSED OPPORTUNITIES FOR REVENUE

The interagency pass program administered by NPS offers five types of "America the Beautiful: The National Parks and Federal Recreational Lands" passes to the public. Four of the passes are specifically designated in FLREA: the Annual Pass, the Age Discount Pass (Senior Pass), the Disability Discount Pass (Access Pass), and the Volunteer Pass. FLREA also outlines other types of passes the Secretary of the Interior may establish, such as site-specific passes, regional multi-entity passes, and discounted- or free-admission days or use. The Military Pass currently falls under this last group. Combined, close to a million of these passes were issued in 2012 (Figure 3).

| America the Beautiful Pass Series | | | |
|---|---|---|---|
| **Pass** | **Price** | **Eligibility** | **Number Issued in 2012** |
| Annual Pass | $80 per year | Available to everyone | 262,678 |
| Military Pass | Free | Available to U.S. military members and dependents | 131,129* |
| Senior Pass† | $10 (lifetime) | Available to citizens and permanent residents age 62 or over | 500,446 |
| Access Pass† | Free | Available to citizens and permanent residents with permanent disabilities | 62,340 |
| Volunteer Pass | Free | Available to volunteers with 250 or more service hours with the five participating FLREA agencies | 1,918 |
| | | **Total** | **958,511** |

* This pass was launched in May 2012. This number represents only passes issued between May and December.

† An additional $10 processing fee is charged for these passes when purchasing by mail.

Figure 3. America the Beautiful pass eligibility and number of passes issued in 2012. Source: NPS staff.

The prices of two of the passes, the $10 Senior Pass and the free Access Pass, are specified in FLREA and may not be changed unless the law is amended. (Park units sold over $5 million in Senior Passes in both 2012 and 2013 and issued over 60,000 Access Passes in 2012 alone.) The fact that changing the fees for these passes would require legislative intervention hampers agencies' flexibility and their ability to make business decisions that would accommodate changing economic conditions and balance visitors' needs with recreation management priorities.

By contrast, NPS can, in its role as interagency pass program coordinator, set the price for the Annual Pass. The current price of the Annual Pass is based on an NPS-contracted analysis from 2006. We understand that NPS is about to undergo another analysis of the interagency pass program and believe that this analysis may be an opportunity to reevaluate the price.

**Recommendations**

We recommend that NPS:

4. Assess the current $80 price for the interagency Annual Pass and update the price accordingly.

## NPS Has Not Updated Its Commercial Bus Tour Fee Schedule Since 1998

NPS' current commercial tour fee schedule, which is based on vehicle size and passenger capacity, became effective January 1, 1998 (Appendix 5). Despite the allowance under LWCFA for periodic adjustments, as of the date of this report the schedule has not been updated in 16 years. Program management staff estimate that NPS could see about $4 million to $5 million in additional revenue by increasing commercial bus tour rates by roughly 30 percent (Appendix 3).

**Recommendations**

We recommend that NPS:

5. Update its commercial tour fee schedule.

## Only Interim Guidance Is in Place for Managing Commercial Use Authorizations

Though not specifically within the original scope of our audit, we learned that some park units opt to place commercial bus tour operators on a commercial use authorization (CUA) rather than charge them a fee based on the commercial bus tour schedule. Formerly known as Incidental Business Permit fees, CUA fees are charged to commercial operators that provide services to NPS visitors and are intended to recover the costs of administering the fee. The park unit generally bases the decision of whether to charge the commercial bus tour fee or issue a CUA on the frequency of visits by the tour operator or the extent of visitor services necessitated by the tour.

Currently, NPS has no permanent guidance for how park units should manage CUAs. Consequently, these fees are determined and managed inconsistently across park units, possibly reducing an opportunity for NPS to recover costs. For instance, two park units we visited (Colorado National Monument and Rocky Mountain National Park) charge operators a flat $250 annual CUA fee. Zion National Park, however, recently moved to a sliding scale that ranges from $200 to $500 based on the amount of revenue the operator made in the park the previous year. Finally, Lake Mead charges a $100 application fee plus $880 annually or $440 for 6 months.

In response to a Notice of Potential Findings and Recommendations we issued on May 1, 2014, NPS staff told us that interim guidance for CUAs has been in place since 2005 and that NPS has been developing guidance that will supersede it. Staff told us that the first topic covered in the new guidance would be cost recovery. They emphasized, however, that cost recovery guidance for commercial use is difficult to standardize throughout NPS because it is based on park units' actual costs to maintain the CUA program, monitor businesses, and recover resource protection expenses—all of which can vary across park units.

**Recommendations**

We recommend that NPS:

6. Expeditiously issue permanent guidance for managing commercial use authorizations.

# Conclusion and Recommendations

## Conclusion

The subject of entrance fees at our national parks is a controversial one, balancing NPS' need to provide the public with easy access to outdoor recreation with the need to fund park maintenance projects and visitor services. Therefore, over the years NPS has proven itself reluctant to raise its entrance fees. Uncertainty over whether FLREA will be repealed or reauthorized hampers NPS' flexibility in managing its Recreation Fee Program, including setting and adjusting park fees, which in turn has seemingly provided a disincentive to raise visitor fees. We understand, however, that NPS has begun the process of addressing some of the issues raised in this review. We discuss those efforts below.

NPS faces considerable, persistent fiscal challenges and needs reliable funding to address visitors' needs. Taking action to update fees, rather than working under self-imposed restrictions, helps NPS address its fiscal shortfalls and positions it as a responsible steward of the funding it already has available.

# Recommendations Summary

We issued a draft version of this report to NPS and received responses to our recommendations. Summaries of the responses, as well as our analysis, are below; see Appendix 6 for the full text of the responses. Appendix 7 lists the status of each of our recommendations.

We recommended that NPS:

1. Assess the need for continuing the freeze on fee increases and consider lifting the moratorium to allow park units to begin submitting requests to adjust fees to align with the current fee model.
   *NPS Response:* NPS responded that on August 9, 2014, the Director lifted the fee moratorium and authorized parks to begin soliciting public support for possible entrance fee changes. Regional directors have until March 2015 to submit completed fee-change requests to NPS' Washington Office for approval. If facing significant public controversy over a fee, parks are permitted to not implement the fee,

to delay fee implementation until 2016 or 2017, or to phase in new rates over 3 years.

*OIG Response:* We are pleased that NPS has lifted its fee moratorium. Based on the information provided, we consider this recommendation resolved and implemented.

2. Begin the process of reevaluating the current fee model to determine necessary updates and establish intervals for periodic reviews to ensure the fee model remains up to date.

   *NPS Response:* In conjunction with lifting the fee moratorium, NPS responded that it also updated the 2006 version of its fee model to allow for inflation while maintaining the same ratios between per-person, vehicle, annual pass, and motorcycle rates (Appendix 8). Once parks have reached their correct rates according to the fee model, and if there is continued public support, additional pricing adjustments may be warranted in the future to keep pace with inflation.

   *OIG Response:* Based on the information provided, we consider this recommendation unresolved. NPS did not indicate that it would establish intervals for periodic reviews of the model to ensure that it remains up to date. We also encourage NPS to reevaluate the fee model in the future to possibly reconsider the current fee groupings of park units as the report suggests. We will refer this recommendation to DOI's Office of Policy, Management and Budget (PMB) to track resolution and implementation.

3. Examine the fee-change process to determine where it can be streamlined and change it accordingly.

   *NPS Response:* NPS' August 9, 2014 memorandum lifting the fee moratorium delegated civic engagement approvals to the regional directors, eliminating the need to submit information to the Washington Office twice.

   *OIG Response:* We are pleased to see the request process streamlined and encourage NPS to continue seeking ways to increase the efficiency of this process. Based on the information provided, we consider this recommendation resolved and implemented.

4. Assess the current $80 price for the interagency Annual Pass and update the price accordingly.

   *NPS Response:* The price of the America the Beautiful pass series was set when FLREA passed in 2004. An interagency working group will likely reevaluate the price of the pass when Congress renews FLREA, which is set to expire in 2016.

*OIG Response:* Based on the information provided, we consider this recommendation unresolved, but we acknowledge the efficiency of waiting to assess pass prices until the status of FLREA is known. This also illustrates our concern that legislative uncertainty hampers NPS' flexibility in managing its Recreation Fee Program. We will refer this recommendation to PMB to track its resolution and implementation.

5. Update its commercial tour fee schedule.

   *NPS Response*: NPS has begun the process of developing alternatives to the current rate structure, along with a strategy for industry input. NPS anticipates that a revised schedule could be implemented in early 2017.

   *OIG Response:* We are pleased that NPS has begun the review process for updating its commercial tour fee schedule, and we encourage it to complete the initiative. Based on the information provided, we consider this recommendation to be resolved but not implemented, and we will refer it to PMB to track its implementation.

7. Expeditiously issue permanent guidance for managing commercial use authorizations.

   *NPS Response*: According to NPS, a workgroup has been working on drafting guidance since the spring of 2013. Guidance has been drafted for several areas including cost recovery, limiting the authorizations, requesting financial information, nonprofits, and insurance. NPS stated that it hopes to have this guidance published by October 1, 2015.

   *OIG Response*: Based on the information provided, we consider this recommendation resolved but not implemented, and we will refer it to PMB to track its implementation.

# APPENDIX 1: SCOPE, METHODOLOGY, AND PRIOR AUDIT COVERAGE

## Scope

This audit is part of a larger portfolio of Office of Inspector General work focused on U.S. Department of the Interior (DOI) business processes and operations, identifying revenue opportunities in DOI's revenue-generating programs. Our objective was to identify opportunities where the National Park

Service (NPS) can increase recreation program revenues. We focused on NPS' three largest revenue-generating mechanisms: entrance fees, interagency passes, and commercial bus tour fees.

## Methodology

We conducted this audit in accordance with Generally Accepted Government Auditing Standards. Those standards require that we plan and perform the audit to obtain sufficient, appropriate evidence to provide a reasonable basis for our findings and conclusions based on our audit objective. We believe that the evidence obtained provides a reasonable basis for our findings and conclusions based on our audit objective.

To accomplish our objective, we performed fieldwork from September 2013 through April 2014. We focused our site visits in the Intermountain and Pacific West regions as they account for more than half of all entrance-fee-charging park units (72 out of 131) and contain all 10 of NPS' Group 4 parks (the top tier of entrance fees).

We spoke to recreation fee staff at NPS headquarters, the Intermountain Region, and the Pacific West Region. We also conducted site visits and spoke to the superintendents or fee staff, or both, at the following park units:

- Arches National Park;
- Canyonlands National Park;
- Colorado National Monument;
- Lake Mead National Recreation Area;
- Muir Woods National Monument;
- Pinnacles National Park;
- Rocky Mountain National Park; and
- Zion National Park.

In the spirit of transparency and open dialogue, we also spoke to—

- officials from the Office of Management and Budget who have an interest in recreation fees;
- a bipartisan research team that conducted a public opinion poll concerning the public's view of NPS; and

- a current congressional committee staffer (formerly the manager of the NPS interagency parks pass program) who is working to get the Federal Lands Recreation Enhancement Act (FLREA) reauthorized.

The primary focus of our audit was to identify revenue opportunities as they pertain to park entrance fees, interagency passes, and commercial bus tours. Consequently, we relied on all of the data provided by NPS, including the estimates for potential revenue. We did not evaluate controls over fee collection and accounting activities, as these matters were beyond the intent of our audit objective. Rather, our report presents findings relating to whether NPS' Recreation Fee Program conforms to public policy as established in FLREA, and whether the park units we visited or contacted were in general compliance with key NPS policies on establishing fees and determining fee levels (principally the fee model).

## Prior Audit Coverage

The last time our office conducted an audit related to NPS' recreation fees was in 2002, before the enactment of FLREA ("Recreational Fee Demonstration Program, National Park Service, Bureau of Land Management," Report No. 2002- I-00451).

# APPENDIX 2: SITE VISIT ENTRANCE FEES (AS OF 2012)

| Park Unit<br>Arches National Park | Group<br>3 | Annual<br>Pass $25 | Per Vehicle<br>$10 | Per<br>Person $5 | Motorcycle $5 (per-<br>person fee) |
|---|---|---|---|---|---|
| Canyonlands National Park | 3 | $25 | $10 | $5 | $5 (per-person fee) |
| Colorado National Monument | 2 | $25 | $10 | $5 | $5 |
| Lake Mead National Recreation Area | 2 | $30 | $10 | $5 | $10 |
| Muir Woods National Monument | 2 | $20 | N/A | $7* | N/A |
| Pinnacles National Park† | 2 | $15 | $5 | $3 | $5 |
| Rocky Mountain National Park | 4 | $40 | $20 | $10 | $10 (per-person fee) |
| Zion National Park | 4 | $50 | $25 | $12 | $12 |

Source: National Park Service (NPS) staff.

* Only $5 of this fee is considered a recreation fee under the Federal Lands Recreation Enhancement Act. The remaining $2 is transferred to the California State park that surrounds the monument.

† Previously Pinnacles National Monument. In 2012, Pinnacles received legislative designation as a national park, but NPS' fee model still classifies it as a Group 2 park unit. NPS' fee model is repeated below:

| Group | Annual Pass | Per Vehicle | Per Person | Motorcycle |
|---|---|---|---|---|
| 1 | $20 | $10 | $5 | $5 |
| 2 | $30 | $15 | $7 | $10 |
| 3 | $40 | $20 | $10 | $15 |
| 4 | $50 | $25 | $12 | $20 |

## Appendix 3: Monetary Impact

| Recreation Fee Source | Potential Additional Revenue |
|---|---|
| Entrance Fee Model | $28 million |
| Commercial Bus Tour Fee Model | $4 million |
| Total | $32 million |

## Appendix 4: Comparison of Select Group 2 and Group 4 Park Units

| Park Unit | Annual Pass | Group Per Vehicle | Entrance Fees* Per Person | Motor-cycle | Acreage | Visitors (FY 2012) |
|---|---|---|---|---|---|---|
| Yellowstone National Park | $50 | $25 | $12 | $20 | 2.2 million | 3.4 million |
| Grand Canyon National Park | $50 | $25 | $12 | $20 | 1.2 million | 4.4 million |
| Yosemite National Park | $50 | $25 | $12 | $20 | 747,956 | 3.9 million |
| Lake Mead National Recreation Area | $30 | $15 | $7 | $10 | 1.5 million | 6.3 million |
| Glen Canyon National Recreation Area | $30 | $15 | $7 | $10 | 1.2 million | 2.1 million |

* Based on the National Park Service fee model. Does not reflect actual fees charged.

# APPENDIX 5: COMMERCIAL TOUR FEE SCHEDULE

| Tier | Effective January National Park Unit | 1, 1998 Sedan* (1 – 6 persons) | Van (7 – 15) | Minibus (16 – 25) | Motor coach (26+) |
|---|---|---|---|---|---|
| I | Grand Canyon National Park | $8 per person† | $8 per person† | $8 per person† | $300 † |
| | Grand Teton National Park | $25* | $125 | $200 | $300 |
| | Yellowstone National Park | | | | |
| | Yosemite National Park | | | | |
| II | Big Bend National Park | $25* | $75 | $100 | $200 |
| | Crater Lake National Park | | | | |
| | Death Valley National Park | | | | |
| | Everglades National Park | | | | |
| | Glacier National Park | | | | |
| | Hawaii Volcanoes National Park | | | | |
| | Kings Canyon National Park | | | | |
| | Mesa Verde National Park | $25* | $75 | $100 | $200 |
| | Mt. Rainier National Park | | | | |
| | Olympic National Park | | | | |
| | Rocky Mountain National Park | | | | |
| | Sequoia National Park | | | | |
| | Shenandoah National Park | | | | |
| III | Acadia National Park | $25* | $50 | $60 | $150 |
| | Badlands National Park | | | | |
| | Bandelier National Park | | | | |
| | Bryce Canyon National Park | | | | |
| | Cape Cod National Seashore | | | | |
| | Dinosaur National Monument | | | | |
| | Harpers Ferry National Historical Park | | | | |
| | Joshua Tree National Park | | | | |
| | Lassen Volcano National Park | | | | |
| | Petrified Forest National Park | | | | |
| | Theodore Roosevelt National Park | | | | |
| | Zion National Park | | | | |
| IV | All other parks that charge an entrance fee as vehicles enter the park‡ | $25* | $40 | $40 | $100 |

Source: National Park Service.

* Sedans: Minimum required fee is $25 commercial fee plus the per-person entrance fee for each passenger.

† Exceptions: At Grand Canyon, the commercial rate is $8 per person for 1-to-25-passenger-capacity vehicles, and a flat rate of $300 for over-26-passenger-capacity vehicles.

‡ Parks that charge only per-person fees should not use this schedule.

Note: The commercial fee is based on the manufacturer's original capacity of the vehicle, not on the number of passengers in the vehicle or the passenger capacity of the vehicle after any subsequent retrofitting. Passenger capacity excludes driver.

# APPENDIX 6: RESPONSE TO DRAFT REPORT

**United States Department of the Interior**

NATIONAL PARK SERVICE
1849 C Street, N.W.
Washington, D.C. 20240

IN REPLY REFER TO:
10 (2608)

JAN - 6 2015

Memorandum

To: Assistant Inspector General of Audits, Inspections and Evaluations

From: Director

Subject: Response to Office of Inspector General Draft Audit Report – Review of National Park Service's Recreation Fee Program (Report No. C-IN-NPS-0012-2013)

We have reviewed the Draft report of November 18, 2014. Responses are listed below for each recommendation.

**Recommendation 1**
**Assess the need for continuing the freeze on fee increases and consider lifting the moratorium to allow park units to begin submitting requests to adjust fees to align with the current fee model.**

On August 9, 2014, via a memorandum to the Regional Directors, I lifted the moratorium and authorized the parks to conduct stakeholder outreach through civic engagement to gauge support for possible fee changes to entrance, expanded amenity and special recreation permit fees authorized by the Federal Lands Recreation Enhancement Act (FLREA) of 2004. The standard entrance fee rate schedule was updated from the 2006 version to allow for inflation and maintain the same ratios between the per person, vehicle, annual pass and motorcycle rates that had been developed in 2006. Each Regional Director was instructed to verify that there is general public support for the proposed fee changes at each park. By March of 2015, the Regional Directors are directed to submit the completed package to the Washington Office that includes concurrence with the proposed changes, documentation of thorough civic engagement, comparability worksheets for all expanded amenity fees and all proposed fee rate changes. The package will be reviewed by the Washington Recreation Fee Office and submitted to me for approval. If there is significant public controversy a park may choose not to implement new fees, may phase in the new rates over 3 years, or delay the new rates until 2016 or 2017.

Contact: Washington Office Recreation Fee Manager, (202) 513-7132.

**Recommendation 2**
**Begin the process of reevaluating the current fee model to determine necessary updates and establish intervals for periodic reviews to ensure the fee model remains up to date.**

Once the parks have reached the correct rates in the model, and if there is continued public support, additional pricing adjustments may be warranted in the future to keep pace with inflation.

Contact: Washington Office Recreation Fee Manager, (202) 513-7132.

**Recommendation 3**
**Examine the fee-change process to determine where it can be streamlined and change it accordingly.**

The memorandum lifting the fee moratorium delegated civic engagement approvals to the Regional Directors eliminating the need to submit information to the Washington Office twice. The memo also included instructional materials and a standardized spreadsheet for documentation of civic engagement activities. This will help to streamline the process. 2015 is the first year that the moratorium has been lifted and we anticipate that there will be a significant number of fee increases. We will continue to look for ways to streamline and make improvements to the process.

Contact: Washington Office Recreation Fee Manager, (202) 513-7132.

**Recommendation 4**
**Assess the current $80 price for the Interagency Annual Pass and update the price accordingly.**

When FLREA was passed in 2004 the five cooperating agencies worked together to create policies and pricing for the new America the Beautiful National Parks and Recreational Lands Pass. A study was done to determine the price. Since the law expires in December 2015 and Congress has not acted with new legislation or extension of the current law, the interagency working group has not proposed any change to the price. It is likely with renewed or revised legislation that the price of the pass will be reevaluated.

Contact: Washington Office Recreation Fee Manager, (202) 513-7132.

**Recommendation 5**
**Update its commercial tour fee schedule.**

In 2014 a lead was established to review the current rate structure and related logistics and background. That lead has interviewed the Washington Office Recreation Fee Manager, Deputy Fee Manager and Park Fee Managers to gain an overview of park logistics, bus size capacities, fee collection and tour operator considerations. She also engaged NPS commercial services personnel to gain an understanding of the relationship between the commercial tour fees and the issuance of commercial use authorizations. The lead is in the process of developing alternatives to share with NPS Management along with a civic engagement strategy for vetting it with the commercial bus industry. The Industry has expressed a strong interest to provide input and also has asked for at least an 18-month lead time so that new pricing information can be published in tour brochures and information. We anticipate that a revised schedule could be implemented in early 2017.

Contact: Washington Office Recreation Fee Manager, (202) 513-7132.

**Recommendation 6**
**Expeditiously issue permanent guidance for managing commercial use authorizations.**

The Commercial Services Program has been in the process of drafting guidance since the spring of 2013 when a workgroup was created to craft the language. Guidance has been drafted for several areas of concern including cost recovery, limiting CUAs, requesting financial information, non-profits and insurance. This draft guidance will be reviewed by regional and park personnel before a final draft is reviewed by solicitors and approved.

We are investigating and developing guidance to address recent changes in the interpretation of the law that will change how reasonable fees are established and how the money is spent. We are also investigating bringing bus tour operators into compliance with entrance fee collection and the commercial use authorization requirements for all commercial operators in national park areas. We hope to have this guidance published by October 1, 2015.

If you have any questions about these responses please contact Associate Director, Business Services at (202) 208-5651.

cc: Associate Director, Business Services
Recreation Fee Manager, WASO
Chief of Concessions, WASO

# APPENDIX 7: STATUS OF RECOMMENDATIONS

| Recommendation | Status | Action Required |
|---|---|---|
| 1 and 3 | Resolved and implemented | None |
| 2 and 4 | Unresolved | We are referring these recommendations to the Office of Policy, Management and Budget (PMB) to track their resolution and implementation. |
| 5 and 6 | Resolved but not implemented | We are referring these recommendations to PMB to track their implementation. |

# APPENDIX 8: UPDATED ENTRANCE FEE MODEL (AS OF 2014)

| Group | Annual Pass | Per Vehicle | Per Person | Motorcycle |
|---|---|---|---|---|
| 1 | $30 | $15 | $7 | $10 |
| 2 | $40 | $20 | $10 | $15 |
| 3 | $50 | $25 | $12 | $20 |
| 4 | $60 | $30 | $15 | $25 |

Source: National Park Service.

## End Notes

[1] The usage and distribution of these fees was subsumed under FLREA when FLREA was enacted in 2004.

[2] In addition to traditional recreation activities common at national parks, such as hiking, camping, and scenic driving, many national recreation areas focus heavily on water-based recreation, such as waterskiing, personal watercraft, and boating.

# INDEX

## D



## E



## F



## G

## O



## P



## R



## S